A NEW ENGLAND GIRLHOOD

This classic memoir of American life in pre-Civil War days is completely reproduced from a copy of the first edition. The decoration of the original binding appears on the cover. Included in this edition is a contemporary magazine illustration titled "Scenes in the Life of Lucy Larcom: Pioneer Life in Illinois—Teaching School in a 'Two-Mile' Neighborhood and Factory Life, The Little 'Doffer'."

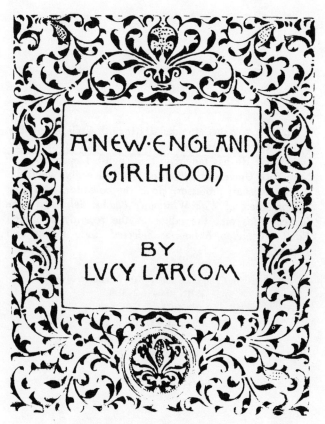

A·NEW·ENGLAND
GIRLHOOD

BY
LVCY LARCOM

Introduction by Charles T. Davis

GLOUCESTER, MASS.

PETER SMITH

1973

CHARLES T. DAVIS attended Dartmouth College and the University of Chicago and received his Ph.D. at New York University. He has taught in the English Departments of New York University and Princeton University, where he is now assistant professor. He is the co-editor, with Gay Wilson Allen, of *Walt Whitman's Poems: Selections with Critical Aids* and the editor of the recently published *Edwin Arlington Robinson: Selected Early Poems and Letters*.

Library of Congress Catalog Card Number: 61-8154

ISBN: 0-8446-2431-4

Copyright © 1961 Corinth Books Inc.

The American Experience Series

Reprinted, 1973, by Permission of
Corinth Books Inc.

INTRODUCTION

If we think of Lucy Larcom at all today, we remember her as one female poet in a steady and sedate procession of others like her extending in the nineteenth century from Sara Josepha Hale and Lydia Huntley Sigourney to Josephine Preston Peabody. One poetess seems to be indistinguishable from another, and all were moral, sentimental, persistently feminist, and limited. Now limited Lucy Larcom's poems certainly are, but they occasionally display a strength which is unusual in the work of these "sweet singers." If we look closely, we see that this power comes from her sensitivity to the physical beauty of her native shore, the Massachusetts coast just below Cape Ann, from her accurate memory of her modest beginnings—as a child in Beverly, a mill-worker at Lowell, and a country teacher in Illinois—and from her sense of the nearness of the past, of that Puritan New England which still existed in many forms around her when she was born in 1824. More impressive in this way than any of her poems, now totally neglected by even the most antiquarian anthologists, is the factual prose record of her early years, *A New England Girlhood, Outlined from Memory*. Miss Larcom published her autobiographical narrative in 1889, four years before her death, with an audience of girls (the "dear girls, for whom these pages have been written") specifically in mind. The author's

awareness of her readers and the simplicity of style which
that awareness enforces contribute charm to Miss Larcom's
story, but the real value of *A New England Girlhood* rests
in its significance as an illuminating document in the
cultural history of nineteenth century America. It is for
this reason that we should read Lucy Larcom again.

Miss Larcom was born early enough (on March 5, 1824,
at Beverly, Massachusetts) to see the fading evidences of
old New England with its close ties to the sea and to the
Congregational meeting-house. Her father, Benjamin, was
a retired shipmaster who came from a family that had
lived near the sea since the arrival in the new world of
Mordecai Larcom in the 1650's. Young Lucy saw everywhere the signs of Yankee sea-faring experience, from
exotic long-handled Chinese fans and Smyrna silks to the
equally exotic faces and features of swarthy foreign visitors from Africa, Asia, and the Pacific islands. Beverly
had much of the country in it, with its closeness to woods,
orchards, wild flowers, and green slopes, but it could not
be provincial while the sea remained alive in the minds
of the people of the village.

Old New England meant also for Lucy Larcom a
proper instruction in Congregational religious practices.
The companion book for the family Bible was the *Westminster Assembly's and Shorter Catechism.* Lucy cele-
brated Election Day, Fast Day, and an austere Christmas,
and she grew up calling "Sunday" the "Sabbath Day"
because it was heathenish to do otherwise.

Lucy Larcom lived long enough to experience most of
the great intellectual challenges that disturbed New England in the nineteenth century and long enough also to
set down in *A New England Girlhood* with sensitivity
and perspective her reaction to the trials that her culture

imposed upon her in the years before 1852. No problem was more important to her than her growing dissatisfaction with the coldness of Calvinist orthodoxy with its emphasis upon "dispensations," "decrees," "ordinances," and "covenants." She loved the old hymns, but yearned for a more intimate and personal relationship with God. It was Emerson who encouraged her to find the spirit of God in the stirring grass of the Illinois prairie and to imagine that her heart lay "bare beneath the piercing eye of the All-Seeing." Though she wrote to a friend in 1858, six years after the terminal action in *A New England Girlhood:* "We all do belong to Christ's Church who love him," [1] Miss Larcom did not find a wholly satisfying religious home until, under the influence of Phillips Brooks, she joined the Episcopal Church in 1890. What is missing in the changing course of her religious life to complete a rough approximation of the major shift in religious thought in New England in the century is only a commitment to Unitarian doctrine.

A New England Girlhood presents an economic crisis in the life of the Larcom family, one which takes us to a radical innovation in the social life of New England. Benjamin Larcom's death forced his widow to take drastic action to seek financial support for her family, and her solution in 1835 was to leave Beverly for Lowell, where she became a housekeeper for a corporation boarding house and Lucy found work in the textile mills. In Lowell Lucy joined girls coming from all over New England to work at the looms and the spinning frames. She encountered the ideals of a new kind of factory, one conceived of by Francis Lowell and Nathan Appleton to depart as widely as possible from old world models. The owners wished to hire girls of education and refinement, including many who looked upon mill work as a way of meeting temporary financial problems, and life at Lowell, with the free grammar school, the church "social circles," the night schools, and the lyceum, contributed to the intellectual and religious development of the mill-girls and nourished a belief in the dignity of labor. Though the Lowell experiment failed finally, when the use of immigrant laborers became widespread in the 1850's, it stands with other noble efforts of the time—Brook Farm, the Fourier phalanx, the Oneida community, and even Thoreau's two years at Walden Pond—which sought to reconcile practical economic solutions and high spiritual aspirations.

Life at Lowell, Miss Larcom tells us, offered the mill-girl a rare opportunity to improve herself. Lucy published for the first time in the *Operatives' Magazine* and became a steady contributor to the *Lowell Offering and Magazine*. She attended classes in German and botany and read widely in English and American literature and history. It was at Lowell too that she met John Greenleaf Whittier and formed the friendship which was the most considerable intellectual relationship in her life. *A New England Girlhood* provides an unusual picture of the American factory system in its youth, when idealism and economic reality attained a momentary balance.

In 1846 Lucy Larcom went west, moved, she says, to settle in a log cabin at Looking-Grass Prairie, Illinois, by "the desire to see the prairies and the great rivers of the West." She shared the impulse felt by many others who had left New England before her, and she sustained herself by following the vocation traditionally associated with New England: she taught school. She continued her education at Monticello Seminary, from which she was graduated in June, 1852.

A New England Girlhood ends in 1852, with Lucy Larcom's return to her native state. The narrative contains few references to her subsequent achievements—as a teacher at Wheaton Seminary at Norton, Massachusetts, as an editor of magazines for young people (*Our Young Folks* and *St. Nicholas*), and as a poet (*The Poetical Works of Lucy Larcom*[2] was published in 1884). We miss too in the autobiography her passionate devotion to the Union cause and the religious speculation of her later years. We have, rather, an account of the growing-up of a New England girl in the early nineteenth century, a record of what she saw, heard, felt, and thought which is of special significance because it reflects, in a most astonishing way, death, birth, frustration, and growth as they emerge in the most influential regional culture of our land.

CHARLES T. DAVIS
Princeton University

1. From a letter to Esther S. Humiston written in the spring of 1858 and published in Daniel Dulany Addison's *Lucy Larcom: Life, Letters, and Diary* (Boston and New York: Houghton, Miffin and Company, 1895), p. 55.

2. Lucy Larcom, *The Poetical Works of Lucy Larcom*, Household Edition (Boston and New York: Houghton, Miffin and Company, 1884). Miss Larcom had published earlier among other works *Poems* (Boston: Fields, Osgood and Company, 1869) and *An Idyl of Work* (Boston: James R. Osgood and Company, 1875), a narrative poem based on her experience in the Lowell mills.

C. T. D.

FACTORY LIFE. THE LITTLE DOFFER

LUCY LARCOM.

A NEW ENGLAND GIRLHOOD

OUTLINED FROM MEMORY

BY

LUCY LARCOM

𝔍 𝖉𝖊𝖉𝖎𝖈𝖆𝖙𝖊 𝖙𝖍𝖎𝖘 𝖘𝖐𝖊𝖙𝖈𝖍

TO MY GIRL-FRIENDS IN GENERAL;

AND IN PARTICULAR

TO MY NAMESAKE-NIECE,

LUCY LARCOM SPAULDING.

Happy those early days, when I
Shined in my angel-infancy!
— When on some gilded cloud or flower
My gazing soul would dwell an hour,
And in those weaker glories spy
Some shadows of eternity : —
Before I taught my tongue to wound
My conscience by a sinful sound ; —
But felt through all this fleshly dress
Bright shoots of everlastingness.

HENRY VAUGHAN.

The thought of our past years in me doth breed
Perpetual benediction.

WORDSWORTH.

PREFACE.

THE following sketch was written for the young, at the suggestion of friends.

My audience is understood to be composed of girls of all ages, and of women who have not forgotten their girlhood. Such as have a friendly appreciation of girls — and of those who write for them — are also welcome to listen to as much of my narrative as they choose. All others are eavesdroppers, and, of course, have no right to criticise.

To many, the word "autobiography" implies nothing but conceit and egotism. But these are not necessarily its characteristics. If an apple blossom or a ripe apple could tell its own story, it would be, still more than its own, the story of the sunshine that smiled upon it, of the winds that whispered to it, of the birds that sang around it, of the storms that visited it, and of the motherly tree that held it and fed it until its petals were unfolded and its form developed.

A complete autobiography would indeed be a picture of the outer and inner universe photographed upon one little life's consciousness. For does not the whole world, seen and unseen, go to the making up of every human being? The commonest personal history has its value when it is looked at as a part of the One Infinite Life. Our life — which is the very best thing we have — is ours only that we may share it with Our Father's family, at their need. If we have anything within us worth giving away, to withhold it is ungenerous; and we cannot look honestly into ourselves without acknowledging with humility our debt to the lives around us for whatever of power or beauty has been poured into ours.

None of us can think of ourselves as entirely separate beings. Even an autobiographer has to say " we " much oftener than " I." Indeed, there may be more egotism in withdrawing mysteriously into one's self, than in frankly unfolding one's life-story, for better or worse. There may be more vanity in covering one's face with a veil, to be wondered at and guessed about, than in drawing it aside, and saying by that act, " There! you see that I am nothing remarkable."

However, I do not know that I altogether approve of autobiography myself, when the subject is a person of so little importance as in the present instance. Still, it may have a reason for being, even in a case like this.

Every one whose name is before the public at all must be aware of a common annoyance in the frequent requests which are made for personal facts, data for biographical paragraphs, and the like. To answer such requests and furnish the material asked for, were it desirable, would interfere seriously with the necessary work of almost any writer. The first impulse is to pay no attention to them, putting them aside as mere signs of the ill-bred, idle curiosity of the age we live in about people and their private affairs. It does not seem to be supposed possible that authors can have any natural shrinking from publicity, like other mortals.

But while one would not willingly encourage an intrusive custom, there is another view of the matter. The most enjoyable thing about writing is that the relation between writer and reader may be and often does become that of mutual friendship ; and friends naturally like to know each other in a neighborly way.

We are all willing to gossip about ourselves, sometimes, with those who are really interested in us. Girls especially are fond of exchanging confidences with those whom they think they can trust ; it is one of the most charming traits of a simple, earnest-hearted girlhood, and they are the happiest women who never lose it entirely.

I should like far better to listen to my girl-readers' thoughts about life and themselves than to be writing out my own experiences. It is to my disadvantage that the confidences, in this case, must all be on one side. But I have known so many girls so well in my relation to them of schoolmate, workmate, and teacher, I feel sure of a fair share of their sympathy and attention.

It is hardly possible for an author to write anything sincerely without making it something of an autobiography. Friends can always read a personal history, or guess at it, between the lines. So I sometimes think I have already written mine, in my verses. In them, I have found the most natural and free expression of myself. They have seemed to set my life to music for me, a life that has always had to be occupied with many things besides writing. Not, however, that I claim to have written much poetry: only perhaps some true rhymes: I do not see how there could be any pleasure in writing insincere ones.

Whatever special interest this little narrative of mine may have is due to the social influences under which I was reared, and particularly to the prominent place held by both work and religion in New England half a century ago. The period of my growing-up had peculiarities which our future history can never repeat, although something far better is undoubtedly already resulting thence. Those peculiarities were the natural development of the seed sown by our sturdy Puritan ancestry. The religion of our fathers overhung us children like the shadow of a mighty tree against the trunk of which we rested, while we looked up in wonder through the great boughs

that half hid and half revealed the sky. Some
of the boughs were already decaying, so that perhaps we began to see a little more of the sky
than our elders ; but the tree was sound at its
heart. There was life in it that can never be lost
to the world.

One thing we are at last beginning to understand, which our ancestors evidently had not
learned ; that it is far more needful for theologians to become as little children, than for little
children to become theologians. They considered
it a duty that they owed to the youngest of us, to
teach us doctrines. And we believed in our in-
structors, if we could not always digest their in-
structions. We learned to reverence truth as
they received it and lived it, and to feel that the
search for truth was one chief end of our being.

It was a pity that we were expected to begin
thinking upon hard subjects so soon, and it was
also a pity that we were set to hard work while
so young. Yet these were both inevitable results
of circumstances then existing ; and perhaps the
two belong together. Perhaps habits of conscientious work induce thought. Certainly, right thinking naturally impels people to work.

We learned no theories about " the dignity of
labor," but we were taught to work almost as if
it were a religion ; to keep at work, expecting
nothing else. It was our inheritance, handed
down from the outcasts of Eden. And for us,

as for them, there was a blessing hidden in the curse. I am glad that I grew up under these wholesome Puritanic influences, as glad as I am that I was born a New Englander; and I surely should have chosen New England for my birthplace before any region under the sun.

Rich or poor, every child comes into the world with some imperative need of its own, which shapes its individuality. I believe it was Grotius who said, "Books are necessities of my life. Food and clothing I can do without, if I must."

My "must-have" was poetry. From the first, life meant that to me. And, fortunately, poetry is not purchasable material, but an atmosphere in which every life may expand. I found it everywhere about me. The children of old New England were always surrounded, it is true, with stubborn matter of fact, — the hand to hand struggle for existence. But that was no hindrance. Poetry must have prose to root itself in; the homelier its earth-spot, the lovelier, by contrast, its heaven-breathing flowers.

To different minds, poetry may present different phases. To me, the reverent faith of the people I lived among, and their faithful everyday living, was poetry; blossoms and trees and blue skies were poetry. God himself was poetry. As I grew up and lived on, friendship became to me the deepest and sweetest ideal of poetry. To live in other lives, to take their power and

beauty into our own, that is poetry *experienced,*
the most inspiring of all. Poetry embodied in
persons, in lovely and lofty characters, more
sacredly than all in the One Divine Person who
has transfigured our human life with the glory
of His sacrifice, — all the great lyrics and epics
pale before that, and it is within the reach and
comprehension of every human soul.

To care for poetry in this way does not make
one a poet, but it does make one feel blessedly
rich, and quite indifferent to many things which
are usually looked upon as desirable possessions.
I am sincerely grateful that it was given to me,
from childhood, to see life from this point of
view. And it seems to me that every young girl
would be happier for beginning her earthly journey
with the thankful consciousness that her life does
not consist in the abundance of things that she
possesses.

The highest possible poetic conception is that
of a life consecrated to a noble ideal. It may be
unable to find expression for itself except through
humble, even menial services, or through unselfish devotion whose silent song is audible to God
alone ; yet such music as this might rise to heaven
from every young girl's heart and character if
she would set it free. In such ways it was meant
that the world should be filled with the true poetry
of womanhood.

It is one of the most beautiful facts in this

human existence of ours, that we remember the earliest and freshest part of it most vividly. Doubtless it was meant that our childhood should live on in us forever. My childhood was by no means a cloudless one. It had its light and shade, each contributing a charm which makes it wholly delightful in the retrospect.

I can see very distinctly the child that I was, and I know how the world looked to her, far off as she is now. She seems to me like my little sister, at play in a garden where I can at any time return and find her. I have enjoyed bringing her back, and letting her tell her story, almost as if she were somebody else. I like her better than I did when I was really a child, and I hope never to part company with her.

I do not feel so much satisfaction in the older girl who comes between her and me, although she, too, is enough like me to be my sister, or even more like my young, undisciplined mother; for the girl is mother of the woman. But I have to acknowledge her faults and mistakes as my own, while I sometimes feel like reproving her severely for her carelessly performed tasks, her habit of lapsing into listless reveries, her cowardly shrinking from responsibility and vigorous endeavor, and many other faults that I have inherited from her. Still, she is myself, and I could not be quite happy without her comradeship.

Every phase of our life belongs to us. The moon

does not, except in appearance, lose her first thin, luminous curve, nor her silvery crescent, in rounding to her full. The woman is still both child and girl, in the completeness of womanly character. We have a right to our entire selves, through all the changes of this mortal state, a claim which we shall doubtless carry along with us into the unfolding mysteries of our eternal being. Perhaps in this thought lies hidden the secret of immortal youth; for a seer has said that " to grow old in heaven is to grow young."

To take life as it is sent to us, to live it faithfully, looking and striving always towards better life, this was the lesson that came to me from my early teachers. It was not an easy lesson, but it was a healthful one ; and I pass it on to younger pupils, trusting that they will learn it more thoroughly than I ever have.

Young or old, we may all win inspiration to do our best, from the needs of a world to which the humblest life may be permitted to bring immeasurable blessings : —

> " For no one doth know
> What he can bestow,
> What light, strength, and beauty may after him go :
> Thus onward we move,
> And, save God above,
> None guesseth how wondrous the journey will prove."
>
> L. L.

BEVERLY, MASSACHUSETTS,
  October, 1889.

CONTENTS.

A NEW ENGLAND GIRLHOOD.

I.

UP AND DOWN THE LANE.

IT is strange that the spot of earth where we
were born should make such a difference to us.
People can live and grow anywhere, but people
as well as plants have their *habitat*, — the place
where they belong, and where they find their happiest, because their most natural life. If I had
opened my eyes upon this planet elsewhere than
in this northeastern corner of Massachusetts, elsewhere than on this green, rocky strip of shore
between Beverly Bridge and the Misery Islands,
it seems to me as if I must have been somebody
else, and not myself. These gray ledges hold me
by the roots, as they do the bayberry bushes, the
sweet-fern, and the rock-saxifrage.

When I look from my window over the tree-
tops to the sea, I could almost fancy that from the
deck of some one of those inward bound vessels
the wistful eyes of the Lady Arbella might be
turned towards this very hillside, and that mine

were meeting hers in sympathy, across the graves
of two hundred and fifty years. For Winthrop's
fleet, led by the ship that bore her name, must
have passed into harbor that way. Dear and gra-
cious spirit! The memory of her brief sojourn
here has left New England more truly consecrated
ground. Sweetest of womanly pioneers! It is as
if an angel in passing on to heaven just touched
with her wings this rough coast of ours.

In those primitive years, before any town but
Salem had been named, this whole region was
known as Cape Ann Side; and about ten years
after Winthrop's arrival, my first ancestor's name
appears among those of other hardy settlers of the
neighborhood. No record has been found of his
coming, but emigration by that time had grown
so rapid that ships' lists were no longer carefully
preserved. And then he was but a simple yeo-
man, a tiller of the soil; one who must have loved
the sea, however, for he moved nearer and nearer
towards it from Agawam through Wenham woods,
until the close of the seventeenth century found
his descendants — my own great - great - grandfather's family — planted in a romantic home-
stead-nook on a hillside, overlooking wide gray
spaces of the bay at the part of Beverly known
as "The Farms." The situation was beautiful,
and home attachments proved tenacious, the family claim to the farm having only been resigned
within the last thirty or forty years.

I am proud of my unlettered forefathers, who were also too humbly proud to care whether their names would be remembered or not; for they were God-fearing men, and had been persecuted for their faith long before they found their way either to Old or New England.

The name is rather an unusual one, and has been traced back from Wales and the Isle of Wight through France to Languedoc and Piedmont; a little hamlet in the south of France still bearing it in what was probably the original spelling — La Combe. There is a family shield in existence, showing a hill surmounted by a tree, and a bird with spread wings above. It might symbolize flight in times of persecution, from the mountains to the forests, and thence to heaven, or to the free skies of this New World.

But it is certain that my own immediate ancestors were both indifferent and ignorant as to questions of pedigree, and accepted with sturdy dignity an inheritance of hard work and the privileges of poverty, leaving the same bequest to their descendants. And poverty has its privileges. When there is very little of the seen and temporal to intercept spiritual vision, unseen and eternal realities are, or may be, more clearly beheld.

'To have been born of people of integrity and profound faith in God, is better than to have inherited material wealth of any kind. And to those serious-minded, reticent progenitors of mine, looking out from their lonely fields across the lonelier sea, their faith must have been everything.

My father's parents both died years before my birth. My grandmother had been left a widow with a large family in my father's boyhood, and he, with the rest, had to toil early for a livelihood. She was an earnest Christian woman, of keen intelligence and unusual spiritual perception. She was supposed by her neighbors to have the gift of " second sight "; and some remarkable stories are told of her knowledge of distant events while they were occurring, or just before they took place. Her dignity of presence and character must have been noticeable.

A relative of mine, who as a very little child, was taken by her mother to visit my grandmother, told me that she had always remembered the aged woman's solemnity of voice and bearing, and her mother's deferential attitude towards her; and she was so profoundly impressed by it all at the time, that when they had left the house, and were on their homeward path through the woods, she looked up into her mother's face and asked in a whisper, " Mother, *was that God?*"

I used sometimes to feel a little resentment at my fate in not having been born at the old Beverly Farms home-place, as my father and uncles and aunts and some of my cousins had been. But perhaps I had more of the romantic and legendary charm of it than if I had been brought up there, for my father, in his communicative moods, never wearied of telling us about his childhood ; and we felt that we still held a birthright claim upon that picturesque spot through him. Besides, it was only three or four miles away, and before the day of railroads, that was thought nothing of as a walk, by young or old.

But, in fact, I first saw the light in the very middle of Beverly, in full view of the town clock and the Old South steeple. (I believe there is an "Old South" in nearly all these first-settled cities and villages of Eastern Massachusetts.) The town wore a half - rustic air of antiquity then, with its old - fashioned people and weather - worn houses; for I was born while my mother-century was still in her youth, just rounding the first quarter of her hundred years.

Primitive ways of doing things had not wholly ceased during my childhood ; they were kept up in these old towns longer than elsewhere. We used tallow candles and oil lamps, and sat by open fireplaces. There was always a tinder - box in some safe corner or other, and fire was kindled by striking flint and steel upon the tinder. What magic it seemed to me, when I was first allowed to strike that wonderful spark, and light the kitchen fire !

The fireplace was deep, and there was a " settle " in the chimney corner, where three of us

youngest girls could sit together and toast our
toes on the andirons (two Continental soldiers
in full uniform, marching one after the other),
while we looked up the chimney into a square of
blue sky, and sometimes caught a snow-flake on
our foreheads ; or sometimes smirched our clean
aprons (high-necked and long-sleeved ones, known
as " tiers ") against the swinging crane with its
sooty pot-hooks and trammels.

The coffee-pot was set for breakfast over hot
coals, on a three - legged bit of iron called a
" trivet." Potatoes were roasted in the ashes,
and the Thanksgiving turkey in a " tin-kitchen,"
the business of turning the spit being usually del-
egated to some of us small folk, who were only too
willing to burn our faces in honor of the annual
festival.

There were brick ovens in the chimney corner,
where the great bakings were done ; but there
was also an iron article called a " Dutch oven,"
in which delicious bread could be baked over the
coals at short notice. And there never was anything that tasted better than my mother's " fire-
cake," — a short-cake spread on a smooth piece
of board, and set up with a flat-iron before the
blaze, browned on one side, and then turned over
to be browned on the other. (It required some
sleight of hand to do that.) If I could only be
allowed to blow the bellows — the very old people called them " belluses " — when the fire began
to get low, I was a happy girl.

Cooking-stoves were coming into fashion, but they were clumsy affairs, and our elders thought that no cooking could be quite so nice as that which was done by an open fire. We younger ones reveled in the warm, beautiful glow, that we look back to as to a remembered sunset. There is no such home-splendor now.

When supper was finished, and the tea-kettle was pushed back on the crane, and the backlog had been reduced to a heap of fiery embers, then was the time for listening to sailor yarns and ghost and witch legends. The wonder seems somehow to have faded out of those tales of eld since the gleam of red-hot coals died away from the hearth-stone. The shutting up of the great fireplaces and the introduction of stoves marks an era ; the abdication of shaggy Romance and the enthrone-ment of elegant Commonplace — sometimes, alas ! the opposite of elegant — at the New England fireside.

Have we indeed a fireside any longer in the old sense ? It hardly seems as if the young people of to-day can really understand the poetry of English domestic life, reading it, as they must, by a reflected illumination from the past. What would the " Cotter's Saturday Night " have been, if Burns had written it by the opaque heat of a stove instead of at his

" Wee bit ingle blinkin' bonnilie ? '

New England as it used to be was so much

like Scotland in many of its ways of doing and
thinking, that it almost seems as if that tender
poem of hearth-and-home life had been written
for us too. I can see the features of my father,
who died when I was a little child, whenever I
read the familiar verse : —

> "The cheerfu' supper done, wi' serious face
> They round the ingle form a circle wide :
> The sire turns o'er, wi' patriarchal grace,
> The big ha' Bible, ance his father's pride."

A grave, thoughtful face his was, lifted up so
grandly amid that blooming semicircle of boys
and girls, all gathered silently in the glow of the
ruddy firelight! The great family Bible had the
look upon its leathern covers of a book that had
never been new, and we honored it the more for
its apparent age. Its companion was the Westminster Assembly's and Shorter Catechism, out of
which my father asked us questions on Sabbath
afternoons, when the tea-table had been cleared.
He ended the exercise with a prayer, standing up
with his face turned toward the wall. My most
vivid recollection of his living face is as I saw it
reflected in a mirror while he stood thus praying.
His closed eyes, the paleness and seriousness of
his countenance, awed me. I never forgot that
look. I saw it but once again, when, a child of
six or seven years, I was lifted to a footstool beside his coffin to gaze upon his face for the last
time. It wore the same expression that it did in

prayer; paler, but no longer care-worn; so peaceful, so noble! They left me standing there a long time, and I could not take my eyes away. I had never thought my father's face a beautiful one until then, but I believe it must have been so, always.

I know that he was a studious man, fond of what was called "solid reading." He delighted in problems of navigation (he was for many years the master of a merchant-vessel sailing to various European ports), in astronomical calculations and historical computations. A rhyming genius in the town, who undertook to hit off the peculiarities of well-known residents, characterized my father as

"Philosophic Ben,
Who, pointing to the stars, cries, Land ahead!"

His reserved, abstracted manner, — though his gravity concealed a fund of rare humor, — kept us children somewhat aloof from him; but my mother's temperament formed a complete contrast to his. She was chatty and social, rosy-cheeked and dimpled, with bright blue eyes and soft, dark, curling hair, which she kept pinned up under her white lace cap-border. Not even the eldest child remembered her without her cap, and when some of us asked her why she never let her pretty curls be visible, she said, —

"Your father liked to see me in a cap. I put it on soon after we were married, to please him;

I always have worn it, and I always shall wear it, for the same reason."

My mother had that sort of sunshiny nature which easily shifts to shadow, like the atmosphere of an April day. Cheerfulness held sway with her, except occasionally, when her domestic cares grew too overwhelming ; but her spirits rebounded quickly from discouragement.

Her father was the only one of our grandparents who had survived to my time, — of French descent, piquant, merry, exceedingly polite, and very fond of us children, whom he was always treating to raisins and peppermints and rules for good behavior. He had been a soldier in the Revolutionary War, — the greatest distinction we could imagine. And he was also the sexton of the oldest church in town, — the Old South, — and had charge of the winding-up of the town clock, and the ringing of the bell on week-days and Sundays, and the tolling for funerals, — into which mysteries he sometimes allowed us youngsters a furtive glimpse. I did not believe that there was another grandfather so delightful as ours in all the world.

Uncles, aunts, and cousins were plentiful in the family, but they did not live near enough for us to see them very often, excepting one aunt, my father's sister, for whom I was named. She was fair, with large, clear eyes that seemed to look far into one's heart, with an expression at once pene-

trating and benignant. To my childish imagination she was an embodiment of serene and lofty
goodness. I wished and hoped that by bearing
her baptismal name I might become like her;
and when I found out its signification (I learned
that "Lucy" means "with light"), I wished it
more earnestly still. For her beautiful character
was just such an illumination to my young life
as I should most desire mine to be to the lives of
others.

My aunt, like my father, was always studying
something. Some map or book always lay open
before her, when I went to visit her, in her picturesque old house, with its sloping roof and tall
well-sweep. And she always brought out some
book or picture for me from her quaint old-fashioned chest of drawers. I still possess the " Children in the Wood," which she gave me, as a
keepsake, when I was about ten years old.

Our relatives form the natural setting of our
childhood. We understand ourselves best and
are best understood by others through the persons
who came nearest to us in our earliest years.
Those larger planets held our little one to its
orbit, and lent it their brightness. Happy indeed
is the infancy which is surrounded only by the
loving and the good!

Besides those who were of my kindred, I had
several aunts by courtesy, or rather by the privilege of neighborhood, who seemed to belong to

my babyhood. Indeed, the family hearthstone came near being the scene of a tragedy to me, through the blind fondness of one of these.

The adjective is literal. This dear old lady, almost sightless, sitting in a low chair far in the chimney corner, where she had been placed on her first call to see the new baby, took me upon her lap, and — so they say — unconsciously let me slip off into the coals. I was rescued unsinged, however, and it was one of the earliest accomplishments of my infancy to thread my poor, half-blind Aunt Stanley's needles for her. We were close neighbors and gossips until my fourth year. Many an hour I sat by her side drawing a needle and thread through a bit of calico, under the delusion that I was sewing, while she repeated all sorts of juvenile sing-song, of which her memory seemed full, for my entertainment. There used to be a legend current among my brothers and sisters that this aunt unwittingly taught me to use a reprehensible word. One of her ditties began with the lines : —

> " Miss Lucy was a charming child ;
> She never said, ' I won't.' "

After hearing this once or twice, the willful negative was continually upon my lips ; doubtless a symptom of what was dormant within — a will perhaps not quite so aggressive as it was obstinate. But she meant only to praise me and please me ;

and dearly I loved to stay with her in her cozy up-stairs room across the lane, that the sun looked into nearly all day.

Another adopted aunt lived down-stairs in the same house. This one was a sober woman; life meant business to her, and she taught me to sew in earnest, with a knot in the end of my thread, although it was only upon clothing for my rag-children — absurd creatures of my own invention, limbless and destitute of features, except as now and then one of my older sisters would, upon my earnest petition, outline a face for one of them, with pen and ink. I loved them, nevertheless, far better than I did the London doll that lay in waxen state in an upper drawer at home, — the fine lady that did not wish to be played with, but only to be looked at and admired.

This latter aunt I regarded as a woman of great possessions. She owned the land beside us and opposite us. Her well was close to our door, — a well of the coldest and clearest water I ever drank, and it abundantly supplied the whole neighborhood.

The hill behind her house was our general playground; and I supposed she owned that, too, since through her dooryard, and over her stone wall, was our permitted thoroughfare thither. I imagined that those were her buttercups that we gathered when we got over the wall, and held under each other's chin, to see, by the reflection, who

was fond of butter; and surely the yellow toad-
flax (we called it "lady's slipper") that grew in
the rock-crevices was hers, for we found it no-
where else.

The blue gill-over-the-ground unmistakably belonged to her, for it carpeted an unused trian-
gular corner of her garden inclosed by a leaning
fence gray and gold with sea-side lichens. Its
blue was beautiful, but its pungent earthy odor —
I can smell it now — repelled us from the damp
corner where it grew. It made us think of graves
and ghosts; and I think we were forbidden to go
there. We much preferred to sit on the sunken
curbstones, in the shade of the broad-leaved bur-
docks, and shape their spiny balls into chairs and
cradles and sofas for our dollies, or to "play
school" on the doorsteps, or to climb over the
wall, and feel the freedom of the hill.

We were a neighborhood of large families, and
most of us enjoyed the privilege of "a little wholesome neglect." Our tether was a long one, and
when, grown a little older, we occasionally asked
to have it lengthened, a maternal "I don't care"
amounted to almost unlimited liberty.

The hill itself was well-nigh boundless in its
capacities for juvenile occupation. Besides its
miniature precipices, that walled in some of the
neighbors' gardens, and its slanting slides, worn
smooth by the feet of many childish generations,
there were partly quarried ledges, which had

shaped themselves into rock-stairs, carpeted with lovely mosses, in various patterns. These were the winding ways up our castle-towers, with break-fast-rooms and boudoirs along the landings, where we set our tables for expected guests with bits of broken china, and left our numerous rag-children tucked in asleep under mullein-blankets or plantain-coverlets, while we ascended to the topmost turret to watch for our ships coming in from sea.

For leagues of ocean were visible from the tip-top of the ledge, a tiny cleft peak that held always a little rain-pool for thirsty birds that now and then stopped as they flew over, to dip their beaks and glance shyly at us, as if they wished to share our games. We could see the steeples and smokes of Salem in the distance, and the hill, as it descended, lost itself in mowing fields that slid again into the river. Beyond that was Rial Side and Folly Hill, and they looked so very far off!

They called it "over to Green's" across the river. I thought it was because of the thick growth of dark green junipers, that covered the cliff-side down to the water's edge; but they were only giving the name of the farmer who owned the land. Whenever there was an unusual barking of dogs in the distance, they said it was "over to Green's." That barking of dogs made the place seem very mysterious to me.

Our lane ran parallel with the hill and the

mowing fields, and down our lane we were always free to go.   It was a genuine lane, all ups and downs, and too narrow for a street, although at last they have leveled it and widened it, and made a commonplace thoroughfare of it.   I am glad that my baby life knew it in all its queer, original irregularities, for it seemed to have a character of its own, like many of its inhabitants, all the more charming because it was unlike anything but itself.   The hill, too, is lost now, buried under houses.

Our lane came to an end at some bars that let us into another lane, — or rather a footpath or cowpath, bordered with cornfields and orchards. We were still on home ground, for my father's vegetable garden and orchard were here.   After a long straight stretch, the path suddenly took an abrupt turn, widening into a cart road, then to a tumble-down wharf, and there was the river!

An "arm of the sea" I was told that our river was, and it did seem to reach around the town and hold it in a liquid embrace.   Twice a day the tide came in and filled its muddy bed with a sparkling flood.   So it was a river only half the time, but at high tide it was a river indeed; all that a child could wish, with its boats and its sloops, and now and then that most available craft for a crew of children — a gundalow.   We easily transformed the spelling into "gondola," and in fancy were afloat on Venetian waters, un-

der some overhanging balcony, perhaps at the
very Palace of the Doges, — willingly blind to
the reality of a mudscow leaning against some
rickety wharf posts, covered with barnacles.

Sometimes a neighbor boy who was the fortunate
owner of a boat would row us down the river —
a fearful, because a forbidden, joy. The widening
waters made us tremble with dread and longing
for what might be beyond; for when we had
passed under the piers of the bridge, the estuary
broadened into the harbor and the open sea.
Then somebody on board would tell a story of
children who had drifted away beyond the harbor-bar and the light-house, and were drowned ;
and our boyish helmsman would begin to look
grave and anxious, and would turn his boat and
row us back swiftly to the safe gundalow and
tumbledown wharf.

The cars rush into the station now, right over
our riverside playground. I can often hear the
mirthful shout of boys and girls under the shriek
of the steam whistle. No dream of a railroad
had then come to the quiet old town, but it was a
wild train of children that ran homeward in the
twilight up the narrow lane, with wind-shod feet,
and hair flying like the manes of young colts, and
light hearts bounding to their own footsteps. How
good and dear our plain, two-story dwelling-house
looked to us as we came in sight of it, and what
sweet odors stole out to meet us from the white-

fenced inclosure of our small garden, — from peach-trees and lilac-bushes in bloom, from bergamot and balm and beds of camomile!

Sometimes we would find the pathetic figure of white-haired Larkin Moore, the insane preacher, his two canes laid aside, waiting in our dooryard for any audience that he could gather : boys and girls were as welcome as anybody. He would seat us in a row on the green slope, and give us a half hour or so of incoherent exhortation, to which we attended respectfully, if not reverently ; for his whole manner showed that, though demented, he was deeply in earnest. He seemed there in the twilight like a dazed angel who had lost his way, and had half forgotten his errand, which yet he must try to tell to anybody who would listen.

I have heard my mother say that sometimes he would ask if he might take her baby in his arms and sing to it; and that though she was half afraid herself, the baby — I like to fancy I was that baby — seemed to enjoy it, and played gleefully with the old man's flowing gray locks.

Good Larkin Moore was well known through the two neighboring counties, Essex and Middlesex. We saw him afterwards on the banks of the Merrimack. He always wore a loose calico tunic over his trousers; and, when the mood came upon him, he started off with two canes, — seeming to think he could travel faster as a quadruped than as a biped. He was entirely harmless; his only wish was to preach or to sing.

A characteristic anecdote used to be told of him: that once, as a stage-coach containing only a few passengers passed him on the road, he asked the favor of a seat on the top, and was refused. There were many miles between him and his destination. But he did not upbraid the ungracious driver; he only swung his two canes a little more briskly, and kept abreast of the horses all the way, entering the town side by side with the inhospitable vehicle — a running reproach to the churl on the box.

There was another wanderer, a blind woman, whom my mother treated with great respect on her annual pilgrimages. She brought with her some printed rhymes to sell, purporting to be composed by herself, and beginning with the verse: —

> "I, Nancy Welch, was born and bred
> In Essex County, Marblehead.
> And when I was an infant quite
> The Lord deprived me of my sight."

I labored under the delusion that blindness was a sort of insanity, and I used to run away when this pilgrim came, for she was not talkative, like Larkin Moore. I fancied she disliked children, and so I shrank from her.

There were other odd estrays going about, who were either well known, or could account for themselves. The one human phenomenon that filled

us little ones with mortal terror was an unknown
"man with a pack on his back." I do not know
what we thought he would do with us, but the
sight of one always sent us breathless with fright
to the shelter of the maternal wing. I did not at
all like the picture of Christian on his way to the
wicket-gate, in " Pilgrim's Progress," before I had
read the book, because he had "a pack on his
back." But there was really nothing to be afraid
of in those simple, honest old times. I suppose
we children would not have known how happy
and safe we were, in our secluded lane, if we had
not conjured up a few imaginary fears.

Long as it is since the rural features of our
lane were entirely obliterated, my feet often go
back and press, in memory, its grass-grown bor-
ders, and in delight and liberty I am a child
again. Its narrow limits were once my whole
known world. Even then it seemed to me as if
it might lead everywhere ; and it was indeed but
the beginning of a road which must lengthen and
widen beneath my feet forever.

II.

SCHOOLROOM AND MEETING-HOUSE.

THERE were only two or three houses between ours and the main street, and then our lane came out directly opposite the finest house in town, a three - story edifice of brick, painted white, the "Colonel's" residence. There was a spacious garden behind it, from which we caught glimpses and perfumes of unknown flowers. Over its high walls hung boughs of splendid great yellow sweet apples, which, when they fell on the outside, we children considered as our perquisites. When I first read about the apples of the Hesperides, my idea of them was that they were like the Colonel's "pumpkin-sweetings."

Beyond the garden were wide green fields which reached eastward down to the beach. It was one of those large old estates which used to give to the very heart of our New England coast-towns a delightful breeziness and roominess.

A coach-and-pair was one of the appurtenances of this estate, with a coachman on the box ; and when he took the family out for an airing we small children thought it was a sort of Cinderella-spectacle, prepared expressly for us.

It was not, however, quite so interesting as the
Boston stage - coach, that rolled regularly every
day past the head of our lane into and out of its
head - quarters, a big, unpainted stable close at
hand. This stage-coach, in our minds, meant the
city, — twenty miles off; an immeasurable distance to us then. Even our elders did not go
there very often.

In those early days, towns used to give each
other nicknames, like school-boys. Ours was called
" Bean-town " ; not because it was especially devoted to the cultivation of this leguminous edible,
but probably because it adhered a long time to
the Puritanic custom of saving Sunday-work by
baking beans on Saturday evening, leaving them
in the oven over night. After a while, as families left off heating their ovens, the bean - pots
were taken by the village baker on Saturday afternoon, who returned them to each house early
on Sunday morning, with the pan of brown
bread that went with them. The jingling of the
baker's bells made the matter a public one.

The towns through which our stage - coach
passed sometimes called it the " bean-pot." The
Jehu who drove it was something of a wag.
Once, coming through Charlestown, while waiting
in the street for a resident passenger, he was
hailed by another resident who thought him ob-
structing the passage, with the shout, —

" Halloo there ! Get your old bean-pot out of
the way ! "

" I will, when I have got my pork in," was the ready reply. What the sobriquet of Charlestown was, need not be explained.

We had a good opportunity to watch both coaches, as my father's shop was just at the head of the lane, and we went to school up-stairs in the same building. After he left off going to sea, — before my birth, — my father took a store for the sale of what used to be called " West India goods," and various other domestic commodities.

The school was kept by a neighbor whom everybody called " Aunt Hannah." It took in all the little ones about us, no matter how young they were, provided they could walk and talk, and were considered capable of learning their letters.

A ladder-like flight of stairs on the outside of the house led up to the schoolroom, and another flight, also outside, took us down into a bit of a garden, where grew tansy and spearmint and southernwood and wormwood, and, among other old - fashioned flowers, an abundance of many-tinted four o'clocks, whose regular afternoon-opening just at the close of school, was a daily wonder to us babies. From the schoolroom window we could watch the slow hands of the town clock, and get a peep at what was going on in the street, although there was seldom anybody in sight except the Colonel's gardener or coachman, going into or out of the driveway directly opposite. It was a very still street; the front win-

dows of the houses were generally closed, and a
few military-looking Lombardy poplars stood like
sentinels on guard before them.

Another shop — a very small one — joined my
father's, where three shoemakers, all of the same
name — the name our lane went by — sat at their
benches and plied their " waxed ends." One of
them, an elderly man, tall and erect, used to come
out regularly every day, and stand for a long time
at the corner, motionless as a post, with his nose
and chin pointing skyward, usually to the north-
east. I watched his face with wonder, for it was
said that " Uncle John " was " weatherwise," and
knew all the secrets of the heavens.

Aunt Hannah's schoolroom and " our shop "
are a blended memory to me. As I was only a
baby when I began to go to school, I was often
sent down-stairs for a half hour's recreation not
permitted to the older ones. I think I looked
upon both school and shop entirely as places of
entertainment for little children.

The front shop-window was especially interesting to us children, for there were in it a few glass
jars containing sticks of striped barley-candy, and
red and white peppermint-drops, and that delect-
able achievement of the ancient confectioner's
art, the " Salem gibraltar." One of my first recollections of my father is connected with that window. He had taken me into the shop with him
after dinner, — I was perhaps two years old, —

and I was playing beside him on the counter when one of his old sea-comrades came in, whom we knew as " Captain Cross." The Captain tried to make friends with me, and, to seal the bond, asked my father to take down from its place of exhibition a strip of red peppermints dropped on white paper, in a style I particularly admired, which he twisted around my neck, saying, —

"Now I 've bought you! Now you are my girl. Come, go home with me!"

His words sounded as if he meant them. I took it all in earnest, and ran, scared and screaming, to my father, dashing down the sugar-plums I wanted so much, and refusing even to bestow a glance upon my amused purchaser. My father pacified me by taking me on his shoulders and carrying me " pickaback " up and down the shop, and I clung to him in the happy consciousness that I belonged to him, and that he would not let anybody else have me; though I did not feel quite easy until Captain Cross disappeared. I suppose that this little incident has always remained in my memory because it then for the first time became a fact in my consciousness that my father really loved me as I loved him. He was not at all a demonstrative man, and any petting that he gave us children could not fail to make a permanent impression.

I think that must have been also the last special attention I received from him, for a little sister appeared soon after, whose coming was announced to me with the accompaniment of certain mysterious hints about my nose being out of joint. I examined that feature carefully in the looking-glass, but could not discover anything unusual about it. It was quite beyond me to imagine that our innocent little baby could have anything to do with the possible disfigurement of my face, but she did absorb the fondness of the whole family, myself included, and she became my father's playmate and darling, the very apple of his eye. I used sometimes to wish I were a baby too, so that he would notice me, but gradually I accepted the situation.

Aunt Hannah used her kitchen or her sitting-room for a schoolroom, as best suited her convenience. We were delighted observers of her culinary operations and other employments. If a baby's head nodded, a little bed was made for it on a soft " comforter " in the corner, where it had its nap out undisturbed. But this did not often happen ; there were so many interesting things going on that we seldom became sleepy.

Aunt Hannah was very kind and motherly, but she kept us in fear of her ferule, which indicated to us a possibility of smarting palms. This ferule was shaped much like the stick with which she stirred her hasty pudding for dinner, — I thought it was the same, — and I found myself caught in a whirlwind of family laughter by reporting at home that "Aunt Hannah punished the scholars with the pudding-stick."

There was one colored boy in school, who did not sit on a bench, like the rest, but on a block of wood that looked like a backlog turned endwise. Aunt Hannah often called him a " blockhead," and I supposed it was because he sat on that block. Sometimes, in his absence, a boy was made to sit in his place for punishment, for being a " blockhead " too, as I imagined. I hoped I should never be put there. Stupid little girls received a different treatment, — an occasional rap on the head with the teacher's thimble; accompanied with a half - whispered, impatient ejaculation, which sounded very much like " Numskull! " I think this was a rare occurrence, however, for she was a good-natured, much-enduring woman.

One of our greatest school pleasures was to watch Aunt Hannah spinning on her flax-wheel, wetting her thumb and forefinger at her lips to twist the thread, keeping time, meanwhile, to some quaint old tune with her foot upon the treadle.

A verse of one of her hymns, which I never heard anybody else sing, resounds in the farthest corner of my memory yet : —

> " Whither goest thou, pilgrim stranger,
> Wandering through this lowly vale ?
> Knowest thou not 't is full of danger ?
> And will not thy courage fail ? "

Then a little pause, and the refrain of the answer

broke in with a change, quick and jubilant, the
treadle moving more rapidly, also : —

> " No, I 'm bound for the kingdom !
> Will you go to glory with me ?
> Hallelujah !   Praise the Lord ! "

I began to go to school when I was about two
years old, as other children about us did. The
mothers of those large families had to resort to
some means of keeping their little ones out of
mischief, while they attended to their domestic du-
ties. Not much more than that sort of temporary
guardianship was expected of the good dame who
had us in charge.

But I learned my letters in a few days, standing at Aunt Hannah's knee while she pointed
them out in the spelling-book with a pin, skipping
over the " a b abs " into words of one and two syl-
lables, thence taking a flying leap into the New
Testament, in which there is concurrent family
testimony that I was reading at the age of two
years and a half. Certain it is that a few passages in the Bible, whenever I read them now,
do not fail to bring before me a vision of Aunt
Hannah's somewhat sternly smiling lips, with her
spectacles just above them, far down on her nose,
encouraging me to pronounce the hard words. I
think she tried to choose for me the least difficult
verses, or perhaps those of which she was herself especially fond. Those which I distinctly recall are the Beatitudes, the Twenty-third Psalm,

parts of the first and fourteenth chapters of the Gospel of St. John, and the thirteenth chapter of the First Epistle to the Corinthians.

I liked to say over the "Blessèds," — the shortest ones best, — about the meek and the pure in heart; and the two "In the beginnings," both in Genesis and John. Every child's earliest and proudest Scriptural conquest in school was, almost as a matter of course, the first verse in the Bible.

But the passage which I learned first, and most delighted to repeat after Aunt Hannah, — I think it must have been her favorite too, — was, "Let not your heart be troubled. In my Father's house are many mansions."

The Voice in the Book seemed so tender! Somebody was speaking who had a heart, and who knew that even a little child's heart was sometimes troubled. And it was a Voice that called us somewhere; to the Father's house, with its many mansions, so sunshiny and so large.

It was a beautiful vision that came to me with the words, — I could see it best with my eyes shut, — a great, dim Door standing ajar, opening out of rosy morning mists, overhung with swaying vines and arching boughs that were full of birds; and from beyond the Door, the ripple of running waters, and the sound of many happy voices, and above them all the One Voice that was saying, "I go to prepare a place for you." The vision gave me a sense of freedom, fearless and infinite. What was there to be afraid of anywhere? Even we little children could see the open door of our Father's house. We were playing around its threshold now, and we need never wander out of sight of it. The feeling was a vague one, but it was like a remembrance. The spacious mansions were not far away. They were my home. I had known them, and should return to them again.

This dim half-memory, which perhaps comes to all children, I had felt when younger still, almost before I could walk. Sitting on the floor in a square of sunshine made by an open window, the leaf-shadows from great boughs outside dancing and wavering around me, I seemed to be talking to them and they to me in unknown tongues, that left within me an ecstasy yet unforgotten. Those shadows had brought a message to me from an unseen Somewhere, which my baby heart was to keep forever. The wonder of that moment often returns. Shadow-traceries of bough and leaf still seem to me like the hieroglyphics of a lost language.

The stars brought me the same feeling. I remember the surprise they were to me, seen for the first time. One evening, just before I was put to bed, I was taken in somebody's arms — my sister's, I think — outside the door, and lifted up under the dark, still, clear sky, splendid with stars, thicker and nearer earth than they have

ever seemed since. All my little being shaped itself into a subdued, delighted " Oh ! " And then
the exultant thought flitted through the mind of
the reluctant child, as she was carried in, " Why,
that is the roof of the house I live in." After
that I always went to sleep happier for the feeling that the stars were outside there in the dark,
though I could not see them.

I did firmly believe that I came from some
other country to this ; I had a vague notion that
we were all here on a journey, — that this was
not the place where we really belonged. Some of
the family have told me that before I could talk
plainly, I used to run about humming the sentence —

> " My father and mother
> Shall come unto the land,"

sometimes varying it with, —

> " My brothers and sisters
> Shall come unto the land ; "

Nobody knew where I had caught the words,
but I chanted them so constantly that my brother
wrote them down, with chalk, on the under side
of a table, where they remained for years. My
thought about that other land may have been
only a baby's dream ; but the dream was very
real to me. I used to talk, in sober earnest,
about what happened " before I was a little girl,
and came here to live " ; and it did seem to me
as if I remembered.

But I was hearty and robust, full of frolicsome health, and very fond of the matter-of-fact world I lived in. My sturdy little feet felt the solid earth beneath them. I grew with the sprouting grass, and enjoyed my life as the buds and birds seemed to enjoy theirs. It was only as if the bud and the bird and the dear warm earth knew, in the same dumb way that I did, that all their joy and sweetness came to them out of the sky.

These recollections, that so distinctly belong to the baby Myself, before she could speak her thoughts, though clear and vivid, are difficult to put into shape. But other grown-up children, in looking back, will doubtless see many a trailing cloud of glory, that lighted their unconscious infancy from within and from beyond.

I was quite as literal as I was visionary in my mental renderings of the New Testament, read at Aunt Hannah's knee. I was much taken with the sound of words, without any thought of their meaning — a habit not always outgrown with childhood. The "sounding brass and tinkling cymbals," for instance, in the Epistle to the Corinthians, seemed to me things to be greatly desired. " Charity " was an abstract idea. I did not know what it meant. But " tinkling cymbals " one could make music with. I wished I could get hold of them. It never occurred to me that the Apostle meant to speak of their melody slightingly.

At meeting, where I began to go also at two

years of age, I made my own private interpretations of the Bible readings. They were absurd enough, but after getting laughed at a few times at home for making them public, I escaped mortification by forming a habit of great reserve as to my Sabbath-day thoughts.

When the minister read, " Cut it down: why cumbereth it the ground? " I thought he meant to say "cu-cumbereth." These vegetables grew on the ground, and I had heard that they were not very good for people to eat. I honestly supposed that the New Testament forbade the cultivation of cucumbers.

And " Galilee " I understood as a mispronunciation of "gallery." " Going up into Galilee " I interpreted into clattering up the uncarpeted stairs in the meeting-house porch, as the boys did, with their squeaking brogans, looking as restless as imprisoned monkeys after they had got into those conspicuous seats, where they behaved as if they thought nobody could see their pranks. I did not think it could be at all nice to " go up into Galilee."

I had an " Aunt Nancy," an uncle's wife, to whom I was sometimes sent for safe-keeping when house-cleaning or anything unusual was going on at home. She was a large-featured woman, with a very deep masculine voice, and she conducted family worship herself, kneeling at prayer, which was not the Orthodox custom.

She always began by saying,—

"Oh Lord, Thou knowest that we are all groveling worms of the dust." I thought she meant that we all looked like wriggling red earthworms, and tried to make out the resemblance in my mind, but could not. I unburdened my difficulty at home, telling the family that "Aunt Nancy got down on the floor and said we were all *grubbelin'* worms," begging to know whether everybody did sometimes have to crawl about in the dust.

A little later, I was much puzzled as to whether I was a Jew or a Gentile. The Bible seemed to divide people into these two classes only. The Gentiles were not well spoken of : I did not want to be one of them. They talked about Abraham and Isaac and Jacob and the rest, away back to Adam, as if they were our forefathers (there was a time when I thought that Adam and Eve and Cain and Abel were our *four* fathers) ; and yet I was very sure that I was not a Jew. When I ventured to ask, I was told that we were all Christians or heathen now. That did not help me much, for I thought that only grown-up persons could be Christians, from which it followed that all children must be heathen. Must I think of myself as a heathen, then, until I should be old enough to be a Christian? It was a shocking conclusion, but I could see no other answer to my question, and I felt ashamed to ask again.

My self-invented theory about the human race was that Adam and Eve were very tall people, taller than the tallest trees in the Garden of Eden, before they were sent out of it; but that they then began to dwindle; that their children had ever since been getting smaller and smaller, and that by and by the inhabitants of the world would be no bigger than babies. I was afraid I should stop growing while I was a child, and I used to stand on the footstool in the pew, and try to stretch myself up to my mother's height, to imagine how it would seem to be a woman. I hoped I should be a tall one. I did not wish to be a diminishing specimen of the race; — an anxiety which proved to be entirely groundless.

The Sabbath mornings in those old times had a peculiar charm. They seemed so much cleaner than other mornings! The roads and the grassy footpaths seemed fresher, and the air itself purer and more wholesome than on week-days. Saturday afternoon and evening were regarded as part of the Sabbath (we were taught that it was heathenish to call the day Sunday); work and playthings were laid aside, and every body, as well as every thing, was subjected to a rigid renovation. Sabbath morning would not have seemed like itself without a clean house, a clean skin, and tidy and spotless clothing.

The Saturday's baking was a great event, the brick oven being heated to receive the flour bread, the flour-and-Indian, and the rye-and-Indian bread, the traditional pot of beans, the Indian pudding, and the pies; for no further cooking was to be done until Monday. We smaller girls thought it a great privilege to be allowed to watch the oven till the roof of it should be " white-hot," so that the coals could be shoveled out.

Then it was so still, both out of doors and within! We were not allowed to walk anywhere except in the yard or garden. I remember wondering whether it was never Sabbath-day over the fence, in the next field; whether the field was not a kind of heathen field, since we could only go into it on week-days. The wild flowers over there were perhaps Gentile blossoms. Only the flowers in the garden were well-behaved Christians. It was Sabbath in the house, and possibly even on the doorstep; but not much farther. The town itself was so quiet that it scarcely seemed to breathe. The sound of wheels was seldom heard in the streets on that day; if we heard it, we expected some unusual explanation.

I liked to go to meeting, — not wholly oblivious to the fact that going there sometimes implied wearing a new bonnet and my best white dress and muslin " vandyke," of which adornments, if *very* new, I vainly supposed the whole congregation to be as admiringly aware as I was myself.

But my Sabbath-day enjoyment was not wholly without drawbacks. It was so hard, sometimes,

to stand up through the " long prayer," and to sit
still through the " ninthlies," and " tenthlies,"
and " finallys" of the sermon! It was impressed
upon me that good children were never restless
in meeting, and never laughed or smiled, however their big brothers tempted them with winks
or grimaces. And I did want to be good.

I was not tall enough to see very far over the
top of the pew. I think there were only three
persons that came within range of my eyes. One
was a dark man with black curly hair brushed
down in " bangs " over his eyebrows, who sat behind a green baize curtain near the outside door,
peeping out at me, as I thought. I had an impression that he was the " tidy-man," though that
personage had become mythical long before my
day. He had a dragonish look, to me ; and I
tried never to meet his glance.

But I did sometimes gaze more earnestly than
was polite at a dear, demure little lady who sat in
the corner of the pew next ours, her downcast
eyes shaded by a green calash, and her hidden
right hand gently swaying a long-handled Chinese
fan. She was the deacon's wife, and I felt greatly
interested in her movements and in the expression of her face, because I thought she represented the people they called " saints," who were,
as I supposed, about the same as first cousins to
the angels.

The third figure in sight was the minister. I

did not think he ever saw me; he was talking
to the older people, — usually telling them how
wicked they were. He often said to them that
there was not one good person among them; but
I supposed he excepted himself. He seemed to
me so very good that I was very much afraid of
him. I was a little afraid of my father, but then
he sometimes played with us children : and besides, my father was only a man. I thought the
minister belonged to some different order of beings. Up there in the pulpit he seemed to me so
far off — oh! a great deal farther off than God
did. His distance made my reverence for him
take the form of idolatry. The pulpit was his
pedestal. If any one had told me that the minister ever did or thought anything that was wrong,
I should have felt as if the foundations of the
earth under me were shaken. I wondered if he
ever did laugh. Perhaps it was wicked for a minister even to smile.

One day, when I was very little, I met the
minister in the street; and he, probably recogniz-
ing me as the child of one of his parishioners,
actually bowed to me! His bows were always
ministerially profound, and I was so overwhelmed
with surprise and awe that I forgot to make the
proper response of a "curtsey," but ran home as
fast as I could go, to proclaim the wonder. It
would not have astonished me any more, if one
of the tall Lombardy poplars that stood along the
sidewalk had laid itself down at my feet.

I do not remember anything that the preacher ever said, except some words which I thought sounded well, — such as " dispensations," " decrees," " ordinances," " covenants," — although I attached no meaning to them. He seemed to be trying to explain the Bible by putting it into long words. I did not understand them at all. It was from Aunt Hannah that I received my first real glimpses of the beautiful New Testament revelation. In her unconscious wisdom she chose for me passages and chapters that were like openings into heaven. They contained the great, deep truths which are simple because they are great. It was not explanations of those grand words that I required, or that anybody requires. In reading them we are all children together, and need only to be led to the banks of the river of God, which is full of water, that we may look down into its pellucid depths for ourselves.

Our minister was not unlike other ministers of the time, and his seeming distance from his congregation was doubtless owing to the deep reverence in which the ministerial office was universally held among our predecessors. My own graven-image worship of him was only a childish exaggeration of the general feeling of grown people around me. He seemed to us an inhabitant of a Sabbath - day sphere, while we belonged to the every-day world.

I distinctly remember the day of my christen-

ing, when I was between three and four years old.
My parents did not make a public profession of
their faith until after the birth of all their children, eight of whom — I being my father's ninth
child and seventh daughter — were baptized at
one time. My two half-sisters were then grown-
up young women. My mother had told us that
the minister would be speaking directly to us, and
that we must pay close attention to what he said.
I felt that it was an important event, and I wished
to do exactly what the minister desired of me. I
listened eagerly while he read the chapter and the
hymn. The latter was one of my favorites : —

"See Israel's gentle Shepherd stands;"

and the chapter was the third of St. Matthew,
containing the story of our Lord's baptism. I
could not make out any special message for us,
until he came to the words, " Whose fan is in his
hand."

That must be it! I looked anxiously at my
sisters, to see if they had brought their fans. It
was warm weather, and I had taken a little one
of my own to meeting. Believing that I was following a direct instruction, I clasped my fan to
my bosom and held it there as we walked up the
aisle, and during the ceremony, wondering why
the others did not do so, too. The baby in my
mother's arms — Octavia, the eighth daughter —
shocked me by crying a little, but I tried to behave the better on that account.

It all seemed very solemn and mysterious to me. I knew from my father's and mother's absorbed manner then, and when we returned from church, that it was something exceedingly important to them — something that they wished us neither to talk about nor to forget.

I never did forget it. There remained with me a sweet, haunting feeling of having come near the " gentle Shepherd " of the hymn, who was calling the lambs to his side. The chapter had ended with the echo of a voice from heaven, and with the glimpse of a descending Dove. And the water-drops on my forehead, were they not from that " pure river of water of life, clear as crystal," that made music through those lovely verses in the last chapter of the good Book?

I am glad that I have always remembered that day of family consecration. As I look back, it seems as if the horizons of heaven and earth met and were blended then. And who can tell whether the fragrance of that day's atmosphere may not enter into the freshness of some new childhood in the life which is to come?

III.

THE HYMN-BOOK.

ALMOST the first decided taste in my life was the love of hymns. Committing them to memory was as natural to me as breathing. I followed my mother about with the hymn-book ("Watts' and Select"), reading or repeating them to her, while she was busy with her baking or ironing, and she was always a willing listener. She was fond of devotional reading, but had little time for it, and it pleased her to know that so small a child as I really cared for the hymns she loved.

I learned most of them at meeting. I was told to listen to the minister; but as I did not understand a word he was saying, I gave it up, and took refuge in the hymn-book, with the conscientious purpose of trying to sit still. I turned the leaves over as noiselessly as possible, to avoid the dreaded reproof of my mother's keen blue eyes; and sometimes I learned two or three hymns in a forenoon or an afternoon. Finding it so easy, I thought I would begin at the beginning, and learn the whole. There were about a thousand of them included in the Psalms, the First, Second, and

Third Books, and the Select Hymns. But I had
learned to read before I had any knowledge of
counting up numbers, and so was blissfully ignorant of the magnitude of my undertaking. I did
not, I think, change my resolution because there
were so many, but because, little as I was, I discovered that there were hymns and hymns. Some
of them were so prosy that the words would not
stay in my memory at all, so I concluded that I
would learn only those I liked.

I had various reasons for my preferences.
With some, I was caught by a melodious echo, or
a sonorous ring; with others by the hint of a picture, or a story, or by some sacred suggestion that
attracted me, I knew not why. Of some I was
fond just because I misunderstood them; and of
these I made a free version in my mind, as I murmured them over. One of my first favorites was
certainly rather a singular choice for a child of
three or four years. I had no idea of its meaning, but made up a little story out of it, with myself as the heroine. It began with the words —

> " Come, humble sinner, in whose breast
> A thousand thoughts revolve."

The second stanza read thus : —

> " I 'll go to Jesus, though my sin
> Hath like a mountain rose."

I did not know that this last line was bad grammar, but thought that the sin in question was

something pretty, that looked "like a mountain-rose." Mountains I had never seen ; they were a glorious dream to me. And a rose that grew on a mountain must surely be prettier than any of our red wild roses on the hill, sweet as they were. I would pluck that rose, and carry it up the mountain-side into the temple where the King sat, and would give it to Him ; and then He would touch me with his sceptre, and let me through into a garden full of flowers. There was no garden in the hymn ; I suppose the "rose" made me invent one. But it did read —

> " I know his courts ; I 'll enter in,
>   Whatever may oppose ; "

and so I fancied there would be lions in the way, as there were in the Pilgrim's, at the "House Beautiful"; but I should not be afraid of them ; they would no doubt be chained. The last verse began with the lines, —

> " I can but perish if I go :
>   I am resolved to try : "

and my heart beat a brave echo to the words, as I started off in fancy on a "Pilgrim's Progress" of my own, a happy little dreamer, telling nobody the secret of my imaginary journey, taken in sermon-time.

Usually, the hymns for which I cared most suggested Nature in some way, — flowers, trees, skies, and stars. When I repeated, —

> " There everlasting spring abides,
>   And never-withering flowers," —

I thought of the faintly flushed anemones and white and blue violets, the dear little short-lived children of our shivering spring. They also would surely be found in that heavenly land, blooming on through the cloudless, endless year. And I seemed to smell the spiciness of bayberry and sweet-fern and wild roses and meadow-sweet that grew in fragrant jungles up and down the hill-side back of the meeting-house, in another verse which I dearly loved : —

> " The hill of Zion yields
> A thousand sacred sweets,
> Before we reach the heavenly fields,
> Or walk the golden streets."

We were allowed to take a little nosegay to meeting sometimes : a pink or two (pinks *were* pink then, not red, nor white, nor even double) and a sprig of camomile ; and their blended perfume still seems to be a part of the June Sabbath mornings long passed away.

When the choir sang of

> " Seas of heavenly rest,"

a breath of salt wind came in with the words through the open door, from the sheltered waters of the bay, so softly blue and so lovely, I always wondered how a world could be beautiful where " there was no more sea." I concluded that the hymn and the text could not really contradict each other ; that there must be something like the sea in heaven, after all. One stanza that I

used to croon over, gave me the feeling of being
rocked in a boat on a strange and beautiful ocean,
from whose far-off shores the sunrise beckoned : —

> " At anchor laid, remote from home,
> Toiling I cry, Sweet Spirit, come!
> Celestial breeze, no longer stay!
> But spread my sails, and speed my way! "

Some of the chosen hymns of my infancy the
world recognizes among its noblest treasures of
sacred song. That one of Doddridge's, beginning
with

> " Ye golden lamps of heaven, farewell! "

made me feel as if I had just been gazing in at
some window of the " many mansions " above. —

> " Ye stars are but the shining dust
> Of my divine abode."

Had I not known that, ever since I was a baby?
But the light does not stream down even into
a baby's soul with equal brightness all the time.
Earth draws her dark curtains too soon over the
windows of heaven, and the little children fall
asleep in her dim rooms, and forget their visions.
That majestic hymn of Cowper's, —

> " God moves in a mysterious way," —

was one of my first and dearest. It reminded me
of the rolling of thunder through the sky; and,
understood as little as the thunder itself, which
my mother told me was God's voice, so that I

bent my ear and listened, expecting to hear it shaped into words, it still did give me an idea of the presence of One Infinite Being, that thrilled me with reverent awe. And this was one of the best lessons taught in the Puritan school, — the lesson of reverence, the certainty that life meant looking up to something, to Some One greater than ourselves, to a Life far above us, which yet enfolded ours.

The thought of God, when He was first spoken of to me, seemed as natural as the thought of my father and mother. That He should be invisible did not seem strange, for I could not with my eyes see through the sky, beyond which I supposed He lived. But it was easy to believe that He could look down and see me, and that He knew all about me. We were taught very early to say " Thou, God, seest me " ; and it was one of my favorite texts. Heaven seemed nearer, because somebody I loved was up there looking at me. A baby is not afraid of its father's eyes.

The first real unhappiness I remember to have felt was when some one told me, one day, that I did not love God. I insisted, almost tearfully, that I did ; but I was told that if I did truly love Him I should always be good. I knew I was not that, and the feeling of sudden orphanage came over me like a bewildering cloud. Yet I was sure that I loved my father and mother, even when I was naughty Was He harder to please than they ?

Then I heard of a dreadful dark Somewhere, the horror of which was that it was away from Him. What if I should wake some morning, and find myself there? Sometimes I did not dare to go to sleep for that dread. And the thought was too awful to speak of to anybody. Baby that I was, I shut my lips in a sort of reckless despair, and thought that if I could not be good, I might as well be naughty, and enjoy it. But somehow I could not enjoy it. I felt sorry and ashamed and degraded whenever I knew that I had been cross or selfish.

I heard them talk about Jesus as if He were a dead man, one who died a great while ago, whose death made a great difference to us, I could not understand how. It seemed like a lovely story, the loveliest in the world, but it sounded as if it were only a story, even to those who repeated it to me; something that had happened far away in the past.

But one day a strange minister came into the Sabbath-school in our little chapel, and spoke to us children about Him, oh! so differently!

"Children," he said, "Jesus is not dead. He is alive: He loves you, and wants you to love Him! He is your best Friend, and He will show you how to be good."

My heart beat fast. I could hardly keep back the tears. The New Testament, then, did really mean what it said! Jesus said He would come back again, and would always be with those who loved Him.

" He is alive ! He loves me ! He will tell me how to be good ! " I said it over to myself, but not to anybody else. I was sure that I loved Him. It was like a beautiful secret between us two. I felt Him so alive and so near ! He wanted me to be good, and I could be, I would be, for his sake.

That stranger never knew how his loving word had touched a child's heart. The doors of the Father's house were opened wide again, by the only hand that holds the key. The world was all bright and fresh once more. It was as if the May sun had suddenly wakened the flowers in an overshadowed wayside nook.

I tried long afterward, thinking that it was my duty, to build up a wall of difficult doctrines over my spring blossoms, as if they needed protection. But the sweet light was never wholly stifled out, though I did not always keep my face turned towards it ; and I know now, that just to let his life-giving smile shine into the soul is better than any of the theories we can invent about Him ; and that only so can young or old receive the kingdom of God as a little child.

I believe that one great reason for a child's love of hymns, such as mine was, is that they are either addressed to a Person, to the Divine Person, — or they bring Him before the mind in some distinct way, instead of being written upon a subject, like a sermon. To make Him real is the only way to make our own spirits real to ourselves.

I think more gratefully now of the verses I learned from the Bible and the Hymn-Book than of almost anything that came to me in that time of beginnings. The whole Hymn-Book was not for me then, any more than the whole Bible. I took from both only what really belonged to me. To be among those who found in them true sources of faith and adoration, was like breathing in my native air, though I could not tell anything about the land from which I had come. Much that was put in the way of us children to climb by, we could only stumble over; but around and above the roughnesses of the road, the pure atmosphere of worship was felt everywhere, the healthiest atmosphere for a child's soul to breathe in.

I had learned a great many hymns before the family took any notice of it. When it came to the knowledge of my most motherly sister Emilie, — I like to call her that, for she was as fond of early rising as Chaucer's heroine : —

"Up rose the sun, and up rose Emilie ; "

and it is her own name, with a very slight change, — she undertook to see how many my small memory would contain. She promised me a new book, when I should have learned fifty; and that when I could repeat any one of a hundred hymns, she would teach me to write. I earned the book

when I was about four years old. I think it was
a collection of some of Jane Taylor's verses. "For
Infant Minds," was part of the title. I did not
care for it, however, nearly so much as I did for
the old, thumb-worn " Watts' and Select Hymns."
Before I was five I had gone beyond the stipu-
lated hundred.

A proud and happy child I was, when I was
permitted to dip a goose quill into an inkstand,
and make written letters, instead of printing
them with a pencil on a slate.

My sister prepared a neat little writing-book
for me, and told me not to make a mark in it
except when she was near to tell me what to do.
In my self-sufficient impatience to get out of "pot-
hooks and trammels" into real letters and words,
I disobeyed her injunction, and disfigured the
pages with numerous tell-tale blots. Then I hid
the book away under the garret eaves, and refused
to bring it to light again. I was not allowed to
resume my studies in penmanship for some months,
in consequence. But when I did learn to write,
Emilie was my teacher, and she made me take
great pains with my p's and q's.

It is always a mistake to cram a juvenile mind.
A precocious child is certainly as far as possible
from being an interesting one. Children ought to
be children, and nothing else. But I am not sorry
that I learned to read when so young, because

there were years of my childhood that came after, when I had very little time for reading anything.

To learn hymns was not only a pastime, but a pleasure which it would have been almost cruel to deprive me of. It did not seem to me as if I learned them, but as if they just gave themselves to me while I read them over; as if they, and the unseen things they sang about, became a part of me.

Some of the old hymns did seem to lend us wings, so full were they of aspiration and hope and courage. To a little child, reading them or hearing them sung was like being caught up in a strong man's arms, to gaze upon some wonderful landscape. These climbing and flying hymns, — how well I remember them, although they were among the first I learned! They are of the kind that can never wear out. We all know them by their first lines, —

"Awake, our souls! away, our fears!"

" Up to the hills I lift mine eyes."

" There is a land of pure delight."

" Rise, my soul, and stretch thy wings,
        Thy better portion trace! "

How the meeting-house rafters used to ring to that last hymn, sung to the tune of "Amsterdam!" Sometimes it seemed as if the very roof was lifted off, — nay, the roof of the sky itself, — as if the music had burst an entrance for our souls into the heaven of heavens.

I loved to learn the *glad* hymns, and there were scores of them. They come flocking back through the years, like birds that are full of the music of an immortal spring!

> " Come, let us join our cheerful songs
> With angels round the throne."
>
> " Love divine, all love excelling;
> Joy of heaven, to earth come down."
>
> " Joy to the world! the Lord is come!"
>
> " Hark! the song of jubilee,
> Loud as mighty thunders' roar,
> Or the fullness of the sea
> When it breaks upon the shore!
>
> " Hallelujah! for the Lord
> God Omnipotent shall reign!
> Hallelujah! let the word
> Echo round the earth and main."

Ah, that word "Hallelujah!" It seemed to express all the joy of spring mornings and clear sunshine and bursting blossoms, blended with all that I guessed of the songs of angels, and with all that I had heard and believed, in my fledgling soul, of the glorious One who was born in a manger and died on a cross, that He might reign in human hearts as a king. I wondered why the people did not sing " Hallelujah " more. It seemed like a word sent straight down to us out of heaven.

I did not like to learn the sorrowful hymns, though I did it when they were given to me as a task, such as —

"Hark, from the tombs,"

and

"Lord, what a wretched land is this,
That yields us no supply."

I suppose that these mournful strains had their place, but sometimes the transition was too sudden, from the outside of the meeting-house to the inside; from the sunshine and bobolinks and buttercups of the merry May-day world, to the sad strains that chanted of "this barren land," this "vale of tears," this "wilderness" of distress and woe. It let us light-hearted children too quickly down from the higher key of mirth to which our careless thoughts were pitched. We knew that we were happy, and sorrow to us was unreal. But somehow we did often get the impression that it was our duty to try to be sorrowful; and that we could not be entirely good, without being rather miserable.

And I am afraid that in my critical little mind I looked upon it as an affectation on the part of the older people to speak of life in this doleful way. I thought that they really knew better. It seemed to me that it must be delightful to grow up, and learn things, and do things, and be very good indeed, — better than children could possibly know how to be. I knew afterwards that my elders were sometimes, at least, sincere in their sadness; for with many of them life must have been a hard struggle. But when they shook their

heads and said, — " Child, you will not be so happy
by and by ; you are seeing your best days now,"
— I still doubted. I was born with the blessing
of a cheerful temperament; and while that is not
enough to sustain any of us through the inevitable sorrows that all must share, it would have
been most unnatural and ungrateful in me to
think of earth as a dismal place, when everything
without and within was trying to tell me that this
good and beautiful world belongs to God.

I took exception to some verses in many of the
hymns that I loved the most. I had my own
mental reservations with regard even to that glorious chant of the ages, —

> " Jerusalem, my happy home,
> Name ever dear to me."

I always wanted to skip one half of the third
stanza, as it stood in our Hymn-Book : —

> " Where congregations ne'er break up,
> And Sabbaths have no end."

I did not want it to be Sabbath-day always. I
was conscious of a pleasure in the thought of
games and frolics and coming week-day delights
that would flit across my mind even when I was
studying my hymns, or trying to listen to the
minister. And I did want the congregation to
break up some time. Indeed, in those bright
spring days, the last hymn in the afternoon always
sounded best, because with it came the opening of

doors into the outside air, and the pouring in of a mingled scent of sea winds and apple blossoms, like an invitation out into the freedom of the beach, the hillsides, the fields and gardens and orchards. In all this I felt as if I were very wicked. I was afraid that I loved earth better than I did heaven.

Nevertheless I always did welcome that last hymn, announced to be sung " with the Doxology," usually in "long metre," to the tune of "Old Hundred." There were certain mysterious preliminaries, — the rustling of singing-book leaves, the sliding of the short screen-curtains before the singers along by their clinking rings, and now and then a premonitory groan or squeak from bass-viol or violin, as if the instruments were clearing their throats ; and finally the sudden uprising of that long row of heads in the " singing-seats."

My tallest and prettiest grown-up sister, Louise, stood there among them, and of all those girlish, blooming faces I thought hers the very handsomest. But she did not open her lips wide enough to satisfy me. I could not see that she was singing at all.

To stand up there and be one of the choir, seemed to me very little short of promotion to the ranks of cherubim and seraphim. I quite envied that tall, pretty sister of mine. I was sure that I should open my mouth wide, if I could only be in her place. Alas ! the years proved that, much as

I loved the hymns, there was no music in me to give them voice, except to very indulgent ears.

Some of us must wait for the best human gifts until we come to heavenly places. Our natural desire for musical utterance is perhaps a prophecy that in a perfect world we shall all know how to sing. But it is something to *feel* music, if we cannot make it. That, in itself, is a kind of unconscious singing.

As I think back to my childhood, it seems to me as if the air was full of hymns, as it was of the fragrance of clover-blossoms, and the songs of bluebirds and robins, and the deep undertone of the sea. And the purity, the calmness, and the coolness of the dear old Sabbath days seems lingering yet in the words of those familiar hymns, whenever I hear them sung. Their melody penetrates deep into my life, assuring me that I have not left the green pastures and the still waters of my childhood very far behind me.

There is something at the heart of a true song or hymn which keeps the heart young that listens. It is like a breeze from the eternal hills ; like the west wind of spring, never by a breath less balmy and clear for having poured life into the old generations of earth for thousands of years ; a spiritual freshness, which has nothing to do with time or decay.

IV.

ALTHOUGH the children of an earlier time heard a great deal of theological discussion which meant little or nothing to them, there was one thing that was made clear and emphatic in all the Puritan training: that the heavens and earth stood upon firm foundations — upon the Moral Law as taught in the Old Testament and confirmed by the New. Whatever else we did not understand, we believed that to disobey our parents, to lie or steal, had been forbidden by a Voice which was not to be gainsaid. People who broke or evaded these commands did so willfully, and without excusing themselves, or being excused by others. I think most of us expected the fate of Ananias and Sapphira, if we told what we knew was a falsehood.

There were reckless exceptions, however. A playmate, of whom I was quite fond, was once asked, in my presence, whether she had done something forbidden, which I knew she had been about only a little while before. She answered "No," and without any apparent hesitation. After the person who made the inquiry had gone, I exclaimed, with horrified wonder, " How could you ? "

Her reply was, " Oh, I only *kind of* said no." What a real lie was to her, if she understood a distinct denial of the truth as only " kind-of " lying, it perplexed me to imagine. The years proved that this lack of moral perception was characteristic, and nearly spoiled a nature full of beautiful gifts.

I could not deliberately lie, but I had my own temptations, which I did not always successfully resist. I remember the very spot — in a foot-path through a green field — where I first met the Eighth Commandment, and felt it looking me full in the face.

I suppose I was five or six years old. I had begun to be trusted with errands; one of them was to go to a farm-house for a quart of milk every morning, to purchase which I went always to the money-drawer in the shop and took out four cents. We were allowed to take a " small brown " biscuit, or a date, or a fig, or a " gibral-tar," sometimes; but we well understood that we could not help ourselves to money.

Now there was a little painted sugar equestrian in a shop-widow down town, which I had seen and set my heart upon. I had learned that its price was two cents ; and one morning as I passed around the counter with my tin pail I made up my mind to possess myself of that amount. My father's

back was turned; he was busy at his desk with
account-books and ledgers. I counted out four
cents aloud, but took six, and started on my errand with a fascinating picture before me of that
pink and green horseback rider as my very own.

I cannot imagine what I meant to do with him.
I knew that his paint was poisonous, and I could
not have intended to eat him; there were much
better candies in my father's window; he would
not sell these dangerous painted toys to children.
But the little man was pretty to look at, and I
wanted him, and meant to have him. It was
just a child's first temptation to get possession of
what was not her own, — the same ugly temptation that produces the defaulter, the burglar, and
the highway robber, and that made it necessary
to declare to every human being the law, " Thou
shalt not covet."

As I left the shop, I was conscious of a certain
pleasure in the success of my attempt, as any thief
might be; and I walked off very fast, clattering
the coppers in the tin pail.

When I was fairly through the bars that led
into the farmer's field, and nobody was in sight, I
took out my purloined pennies, and looked at them
as they lay in my palm.

Then a strange thing happened. It•was a
bright morning, but it seemed to me as if the sky
grew suddenly dark; and those two pennies began to burn through my hand, to scorch me, as if

they were red hot, to my very soul. It was agony to hold them. I laid them down under a tuft of grass in the footpath, and ran as if I had left a demon behind me. I did my errand, and returning, I looked about in the grass for the two cents, wondering whether they could make me feel so badly again. But my good angel hid them from me ; I never found them.

I was too much of a coward to confess my fault to my father ; I had already begun to think of him as " an austere man," like him in the parable of the talents. I should have been a much happier child if I had confessed, for I had to carry about with me for weeks and months a heavy burden of shame. I thought of myself as a thief, and used to dream of being carried off to jail and condemned to the gallows for my offense : one of my story-books told about a boy who was hanged at Tyburn for stealing, and how was I better than he ?

Whatever naughtiness I was guilty of afterwards, I never again wanted to take what belonged to another, whether in the family or out of it. I hated the sight of the little sugar horseback rider from that day, and was thankful enough when some other child had bought him and left his place in the window vacant.

About this time I used to lie awake nights a good deal, wondering what became of infants who were wicked. I had heard it said that all who died in infancy went to heaven, but it was also said that those who sinned could not possibly go to heaven. I understood, from talks I had listened to among older people, that infancy lasted until children were about twelve years of age. Yet here was I, an infant of less than six years, who had committed a sin. I did not know what to do with my own case. I doubted whether it would do any good for me to pray to be forgiven, but I did pray, because I could not help it, though not aloud. I believe I preferred thinking my prayers to saying them, almost always.

Inwardly, I objected to the idea of being an infant; it seemed to me like being nothing in particular — neither a child nor a little girl, neither a baby nor a woman. Having discovered that I was capable of being wicked, I thought it would be better if I could grow up at once, and assume my own responsibilities. It quite demoralized me when people talked in my presence about "innocent little children."

There was much questioning in those days as to whether fictitious reading was good for children. To "tell a story" was one equivalent expression for lying. But those who came nearest to my child-life recognized the value of truth as impressed through the imagination, and left me in delightful freedom among my fairy-tale books. I think I saw a difference, from the first, between the old poetic legends and a modern lie, especially if this latter was the invention of a fancy as youthful as my own.

I supposed that the beings of those imaginative tales had lived some time, somewhere ; perhaps they still existed in foreign countries, which were all a realm of fancy to me. I was certain that they could not inhabit our matter-of-fact neighborhood. I had never heard that any fairies or elves came over with the Pilgrims in the Mayflower. But a little red - haired playmate with whom I became intimate used to take me off with her into the fields, where, sitting on the edge of a disused cartway fringed with pussy-clover, she poured into my ears the most remarkable narratives of acquaintances she had made with people who lived under the ground close by us, in my father's orchard. Her literal descriptions quite deceived me ; I swallowed her stories entire, just as people in the last century did Defoe's account of " The Apparition of Mrs. Veal."

She said that these subterranean people kept house, and that they invited her down to play with their children on Wednesday and Saturday afternoons ; also that they sometimes left a plate of cakes and tarts for her at their door : she offered to show me the very spot where it was, — under a great apple-tree which my brothers called " the luncheon-tree," because we used to rest and refresh ourselves there, when we helped my father weed his vegetable-garden. But she guarded herself by informing me that it would be impossible for us to open the door ourselves; that it could only be unfastened from the inside. She told me these people's names — a " Mr. Pelican," and a " Mr. Apple-tree Manasseh," who had a very large family of little " Manassehs." She said that there was a still larger family, some of them probably living just under the spot where we sat, whose sirname was " Hokes." (If either of us had been familiar with another word pronounced in the same way, though spelled differently, I should since have thought that she was all the time laughing in her sleeve at my easy belief.) These " Hokeses " were not good-natured people, she added, whispering to me that we must not speak about them aloud, as they had sharp ears, and might overhear us, and do us mischief.

I think she was hoaxing herself as well as me ; it was her way of being a heroine in her own eyes and mine, and she had always the manner of being entirely in earnest.

But she became more and more romantic in her inventions. A distant aristocratic - looking mansion, which we could see half-hidden by trees, across the river, she assured me was a haunted house, and that she had passed many a night there, seeing unaccountable sights, and hearing mysterious sounds. She further announced that she was to be married, some time, to a young man who lived over there. I inferred that the marriage was to take place whenever the ghostly tenants of the house would give their consent. She revealed to me, under promise of strict secrecy, the young man's name. It was " Alonzo."

Not long after I picked up a book which one of my sisters had borrowed, called " Alonzo and Melissa," and I discovered that she had been telling me page after page of " Melissa's " adventures, as if they were her own. The fading memory I have of the book is that it was a very silly one ; and when I discovered that the rest of the romantic occurrences she had related, not in that volume, were to be found in " The Children of the Abbey," I left off listening to her. I do not think I regarded her stories as lies ; I only lost my interest in them after I knew that they were all of her own clumsy second-hand making-up, out of the most commonplace material.

My two brothers liked to play upon my credulity. When my brother Ben pointed up to the gilded weather-cock on the Old South steeple, and said to me with a very grave face, —

" Did you know that whenever that cock crows every rooster in town crows too ? " I listened out at the window, and asked, —

" But when *will* he begin to crow ? "

" Oh, roosters crow in the night, sometimes, when you are asleep."

Then my younger brother would break in with a shout of delight at my stupidity : —

"I 'll tell you when, goosie! —

   ' The next day after never ;
   When the dead ducks fly over the river.' "

But this must have been when I was very small ;
for I remember thinking that "the next day
after never" would come some time, in millions of
years, perhaps. And how queer it would be to
see dead ducks flying through the air!

Witches were seldom spoken of in the presence of us children. We sometimes overheard a
snatch of a witch-story, told in whispers, by the
flickering firelight, just as we were being sent off
to bed. But, to the older people, those legends were
too much like realities, and they preferred not
to repeat them. Indeed, it was over our town
that the last black shadow of the dreadful witch-
craft delusion had rested. Mistress Hale's house
was just across the burying-ground, and Gallows
Hill was only two miles away, beyond the bridge.
Yet I never really knew what the "Salem Witch-
craft" was until Goodrich's "History of the
United States" was put into my hands as a school-
book, and I read about it there.

Elves and gnomes and air-sprites and genii
were no strangers to us, for my sister Emilie —
she who heard me say my hymns, and taught me
to write — was mistress of an almost limitless
fund of imaginative lore. She was a very Sche-
herezade of story-tellers, so her younger sisters
thought, who listened to her while twilight grew

into moonlight, evening after evening, with fasci-
nated wakefulness.

Besides the tales that the child-world of all
ages is familiar with, — Red Riding - Hood, the
Giant-Killer, Cinderella, Aladdin, the "Sleeping
Beauty," and the rest, — she had picked up somewhere most of the folk - stories of Ireland and
Scotland, and also the wild legends of Germany,
which latter were not then made into the compact
volumes known among juvenile readers of to-day
as Grimm's "Household Tales."

Her choice was usually judicious; she omitted
the ghosts and goblins that would have haunted
our dreams; although I was now and then visited by a nightmare - consciousness of being a
bewitched princess who must perform some impossible task, such as turning a whole roomful of
straws into gold, one by one, or else lose my head.
But she blended the humorous with the romantic
in her selections, so that we usually dropped to
sleep in good spirits, if not with a laugh.

That old story of the fisherman who had done
the "Man of the Sea" a favor, and was to be rewarded by having his wish granted, she told in so
quaintly realistic a way that I thought it might all
have happened on one of the islands out in Massachusetts Bay. The fisherman was foolish enough,
it seemed, to let his wife do all his wishing for
him; and she, unsatisfied still, though she had
been made first an immensely rich woman, and

then a great queen, at last sent her husband to ask that they two might be made rulers over the sun, moon, and stars.

As my sister went on with the story, I could see the waves grow black, and could hear the wind mutter and growl, while the fisherman called for the first, second, and then reluctantly, for the third time: —

> " O Man of the Sea,
>   Come listen to me!
> For Alice my wife,
>   The plague of my life,
> Has sent me to beg a boon of thee ! "

As his call died away on the sullen wind, the mysterious " Man of the Sea " rose in his wrath out of the billows, and said, —

" Go back to your old mud hut, and stay there with your wife Alice, and never come to trouble me again."

I sympathized with the " Man of the Sea " in his righteous indignation at the conduct of the greedy, grasping woman ; and the moral of the story remained with me, as the story itself did. I think I understood dimly, even then, that mean avarice and self - seeking ambition always find their true level in muddy earth, never among the stars.

So it proved that my dear mother-sister was preparing me for life when she did not know it, when she thought she was only amusing me.

This sister, though only just entering her teens,

was toughening herself by all sorts of unnecessary hardships for whatever might await her womanhood. She used frequently to sleep in the garret on a hard wooden sea-chest instead of in a bed. And she would get up before daylight and run over into the burying-ground, barefooted and white-robed (we lived for two or three years in another house than our own, where the oldest graveyard in town was only separated from us by our garden fence), " to see if there were any ghosts there," she told us. Returning noiselessly, — herself a smiling phantom, with long, golden-brown hair rippling over her shoulders, — she would drop a trophy upon her little sisters' pillow, in the shape of a big, yellow apple that had dropped from "the Colonel's" "pumpkin sweeting" tree into the graveyard, close to our fence.

She was fond of giving me surprises, of watching my wonder at seeing anything beautiful or strange for the first time. Once, when I was very little, she made me supremely happy by rousing me before four o'clock in the morning, dressing me hurriedly, and taking me out with her for a walk across the graveyard and through the dewy fields. The birds were singing, and the sun was just rising, and we were walking toward the east, hand in hand, when suddenly there appeared before us what looked to me like an immense blue wall, stretching right and left as far as I could see.

" Oh, what is it the wall of ? " I cried.

It was a revelation she had meant for me. "So you did not know it was the sea, little girl!" she said.

It was a wonderful illusion to my unaccustomed eyes, and I took in at that moment for the first time something of the real grandeur of the ocean. Not a sail was in sight, and the blue expanse was scarcely disturbed by a ripple, for it was the high-tide calm. That morning's freshness, that vision of the sea, I know I can never lose.

From our garret window — and the garret was my usual retreat when I wanted to get away by myself with my books or my dreams — we had the distant horizon-line of the bay, across a quarter of a mile of trees and mowing fields. We could see the white breakers dashing against the long, narrow island just outside of the harbor, which I, with my childish misconstruction of names, called "Breakers' Island"; supposing that the grown people had made a mistake when they spoke of it as "Baker's." But that far-off, shining band of silver and blue seemed so different from the whole great sea, stretching out as if into eternity from the feet of the baby on the shore!

The marvel was not lessened when I began to study geography, and comprehended that the world is round. Could it really be that we had that endless "Atlantic Ocean" to look at from our window, to dance along the edge of, to wade into or bathe in, if we chose? The map of the world became more interesting to me than any of the story-books. In my fanciful explorations I out-traveled Captain Cook, the only voyager around the world with whose name my childhood was familiar.

The field-paths were safe, and I was allowed to wander off alone through them. I greatly enjoyed the freedom of a solitary explorer among the sea-shells and wild flowers.

There were wonders everywhere. One day I picked up a star-fish on the beach (we called it a "five-finger"), and hung him on a tree to dry, not thinking of him as a living creature. When I went some time after to take him down he had clasped with two or three of his fingers the bough where I laid him, so that he could not be removed without breaking his hardened shell. My conscience smote me when I saw what an unhappy-looking skeleton I had made of him.

I overtook the horse-shoe crab on the sands, but I did not like to turn him over and make him "say his prayers," as some of the children did. I thought it must be wicked. And then he looked so uncomfortable, imploringly wriggling his claws while he lay upon his back! I believe I did, however, make a small collection of the shells of stranded horse-shoe crabs deserted by their tenants.

There were also pretty canary-colored cockle-shells and tiny purple mussels washed up by the tide. I gathered them into my apron, and carried them home, and only learned that they too held living inhabitants by seeing a dead snail protruding from every shell after they had been left to themselves for a day or two. This made me careful to pick up only the empty ones, and there were plenty of them. One we called a "butterboat"; it had something shaped like a seat across the end of it on the inside. And the curious seaurchin, that looked as if he was made only for ornament, when he had once got rid of his spines,— and the transparent jelly-fish, that seemed to have no more right to be alive than a ladleful of mucilage, — and the razor-shells, and the barnacles, and the knotted kelp, and the flabby green seaaprons, — there was no end to the interesting things I found when I was trusted to go down to the edge of the tide alone.

The tide itself was the greatest marvel, slipping away so noiselessly, and creeping back so softly over the flats, whispering as it reached the sands, and laughing aloud "I am coming!" as, dashing against the rocks, it drove me back to where the sea-lovage and purple beach-peas had dared to root themselves. I listened, and felt through all my little being that great, surging word of power, but had no guess of its meaning. I can think of it now as the eternal voice of Law, ever returning to the green, blossoming, beautiful verge of Gospel truth, to confirm its later revelation, and to say

that Law and Gospel belong together. " The sea
is His, and He made it : and His hands formed
the dry land."

And the dry land, the very dust of the earth,
every day revealed to me some new miracle of a
flower. Coming home from school one warm noon,
I chanced to look down, and saw for the first time
the dry roadside all starred with lavender-tinted
flowers, scarcely larger than a pin - head ; fairy-
flowers, indeed ; prettier than anything that grew
in gardens. It was the red sand-wort; but why
a purple flower should be called red, I do not
know. I remember holding these little amethys-
tine blossoms like jewels in the palm of my hand,
and wondering whether people who walked along
that road knew what beautiful things they were
treading upon. I never found the flower open
except at noonday, when the sun was hottest.
The rest of the time it was nothing but an in-
significant, dusty-leaved weed, — a weed that was
transformed into a flower only for an hour or two
every day. It seemed like magic.

The busy people at home could tell me very
little about the wild flowers, and when I found a
new one I thought I was its discoverer. I can
see myself now leaning in ecstasy over a small,
rough-leaved purple aster in a lonely spot on the
hill, and thinking that nobody else in all the
world had ever beheld such a flower before, because I never had. I did not know then, that

the flower-generations are older than the human race.

The commonest blossoms were, after all, the dearest, because they were so familiar. Very few of us lived upon carpeted floors, but soft green grass stretched away from our door-steps, all golden with dandelions in spring. Those dandelion fields were like another heaven dropped down upon the earth, where our feet wandered at will among the stars. What need had we of luxurious upholstery, when we could step out into such splendor, from the humblest door?

The dandelions could tell us secrets, too. We blew the fuzz off their gray heads, and made them answer our question, " Does my mother want me to come home? " Or we sat down together in the velvety grass, and wove chains for our necks and wrists of the dandelion-stems, and " made believe " we were brides, or queens, or empresses.

Then there was the white rock-saxifrage, that filled the crevices of the ledges with soft, tufty bloom like lingering snow-drifts, our May-flower, that brought us the first message of spring. There was an elusive sweetness in its almost imperceptible breath, which one could only get by smelling it in close bunches. Its companion was the tiny four-cleft innocence-flower, that drifted pale sky-tints across the chilly fields. Both came to us in crowds, and looked out with us, as they do with

the small girls and boys of to-day, from the windy
crest of Powder House Hill, — the one playground
of my childhood which is left to the children and
the cows just as it was then. We loved these
little democratic blossoms, that gathered around
us in mobs at our May Day rejoicings. It is
doubtful whether we should have loved the trailing arbutus any better, had it strayed, as it never
did, into our woods.

Violets and anemones played at hide-and-seek
with us in shady places. The gay columbine
rooted herself among the bleak rocks, and
laughed and nodded in the face of the east wind,
coquettishly wasting the show of her finery on
the frowning air. Bluebirds twittered over the
dandelions in spring. In midsummer, goldfinches
warbled among the thistle-tops; and, high above
the bird - congregations, the song - sparrow sent
forth her clear, warm, penetrating trill, — sunshine translated into music.

We were not surfeited, in those days, with
what is called pleasure; but we grew up happy
and healthy, learning unconsciously the useful
lesson of *doing without.* The birds and blossoms hardly won a gladder or more wholesome life
from the air of our homely New England than
we did.

"Out of the strong came forth sweetness."
The Beatitudes are the natural flowering-forth
of the Ten Commandments. And the happiness

of our lives was rooted in the stern, vigorous virtues of the people we lived among, drawing
thence its bloom and song and fragrance. There
was granite in their character and beliefs, but it
was granite that could smile in the sunshine and
clothe itself with flowers. We little ones felt the
firm rock beneath us, and were lifted up on it, to
emulate their goodness, and to share their aspirations.

V.

OLD NEW ENGLAND.

WHEN I first opened my eyes upon my native town, it was already nearly two hundred years old, counting from the time when it was part of the original Salem settlement, — old enough to have gained a character and an individuality of its own, as it certainly had. We children felt at once that we belonged to the town, as we did to our father or our mother.

The sea was its nearest neighbor, and penetrated to every fireside, claiming close intimacy with every home and heart. The farmers up and down the shore were as much fishermen as farmers; they were as familiar with the Grand Banks of Newfoundland as they were with their own potato-fields. Every third man you met in the street, you might safely hail as " Shipmate," or " Skipper," or " Captain." My father's early seafaring experience gave him the latter title to the end of his life.

It was hard to keep the boys from going off to sea before they were grown. No inland occupation attracted them. " Land - lubber " was one of the most contemptuous epithets heard from boyish lips. The spirit of adventure developed in them a rough, breezy type of manliness, now almost extinct.

Men talked about a voyage to Calcutta, or Hong-Kong, or " up the Straits," — meaning Gibraltar and the Mediterranean, — as if it were not much more than going to the next village. It seemed as if our nearest neighbors lived over there across the water; we breathed the air of foreign countries, curiously interblended with our own.

The women of well-to-do families had Canton crape shawls and Smyrna silks and Turk satins, for Sabbath - day wear, which somebody had brought home for them. Mantel - pieces were adorned with nautilus and conch-shells, and with branches and fans of coral; and children had foreign curiosities and treasures of the sea for playthings. There was one imported shell that we did not value much, it was so abundant — the freckled univalve they called a "prop." Yet it had a mysterious interest for us little ones. We held it to our ears, and listened for the sound of the waves, which we were told that it still kept, and always would keep. I remember the time when I thought that the ocean was really imprisoned somewhere within that narrow aperture.

We were accustomed to seeing barrels full of cocoa-nuts rolled about; and there were jars of preserved tropical fruits, tamarinds, ginger-root, and other spicy appetizers, almost as common as barberries and cranberries, in the cupboards of most housekeepers.

I wonder what has become of those many, many little red " guinea-peas " we had to play with! It never seemed as if they really belonged to the vegetable world, notwithstanding their name.

We had foreign coins mixed in with our large copper cents, — all kinds, from the Russian " kopeck " to the " half-penny token " of Great Britain. Those were the days when we had half cents in circulation to make change with. For part of our currency was the old-fashioned " ninepence," — twelve and a half cents, and the " four pence ha'penny," — six cents and a quarter. There was a good deal of Old England about us still.

And we had also many living reminders of strange lands across the sea. Green parrots went scolding and laughing down the thimbleberry hedges that bordered the cornfields, as much at home out of doors as within. Java sparrows and canaries and other tropical song-birds poured their music out of sunny windows into the street, delighting the ears of passing school children long before the robins came. Now and then somebody's pet monkey would escape along the stone walls and shed-roofs, and try to hide from his boy-persecutors by dodging behind a chimney, or by slipping through an open scuttle, to the terror and delight of juveniles whose premises he invaded.

And there were wanderers from foreign countries domesticated in many families, whose swarthy complexions and un-Caucasian features became familiar in our streets, — Mongolians, Africans, and waifs from the Pacific islands, who always were known to us by distinguished names, — Hector and Scipio, and Julius Cæsar and Christopher Columbus. Families of black people were scattered about the place, relics of a time when even New England had not freed her slaves. Some of them had belonged in my great-grandfather's family, and they hung about the old homestead at "The Farms" long after they were at liberty to go anywhere they pleased. There was a "Rose" and a "Phillis" among them, who came often to our house to bring luscious high blackberries from the Farms woods, or to do the household washing. They seemed pathetically out of place, although they lived among us on equal terms, respectable and respected.

The pathos of the sea haunted the town, made audible to every ear when a coming northeaster brought the rote of the waves in from the islands across the harbor-bar, with a moaning like that we heard when we listened for it in the shell. Almost every house had its sea-tragedy. Somebody belonging to it had been shipwrecked, or had sailed away one day, and never returned.

Our own part of the bay was so sheltered by its islands that there were seldom any disasters heard of near home, although the names of the two nearest — Great and Little Misery — are said to have originated with a shipwreck so far back in the history of the region that it was never recorded.

But one such calamity happened in my infancy, spoken of always by those who knew its victims in subdued tones; — the wreck of the " Persia." The vessel was returning from the Mediterranean, and in a blinding snow-storm on a wild March night her captain probably mistook one of the Cape Ann light-houses for that on Baker's Island, and steered straight upon the rocks in a lonely cove just outside the cape. In the morning the bodies of her dead crew were found tossing about with her cargo of paper-manufacturers' rags, among the breakers. Her captain and mate were Beverly men, and their funeral from the meeting - house the next Sabbath was an event which long left its solemnity hanging over the town.

We were rather a young nation at this time. The History of the United States could only tell the story of the American Revolution, of the War of 1812, and of the administration of about half a dozen presidents.

Our republicanism was fresh and wide-awake. The edge of George Washington's little hatchet had not yet been worn down to its latter-day dullness; it flashed keenly on our young eyes and ears in the reading books, and through Fourth of July speeches. The Father of his Country had been dead only a little more than a quarter of a century, and General Lafayette was still alive; he had, indeed, passed through our town but a few years before, and had been publicly welcomed under our own elms and lindens. Even babies echoed the names of our two heroes in their prattle.

We had great " training-days," when drum and fife took our ears by storm; when the militia and the Light Infantry mustered and marched through the streets to the Common, with boys and girls at their heels, — such girls as could get their mother's consent, or the courage to run off without it. We never could. But we always managed to get a good look at the show in one way or another.

" Old Election," " 'Lection Day " we called it, a lost holiday now, was a general training day, and it came at our most delightful season, the last of May. Lilacs and tulips were in bloom, then; and it was a picturesque fashion of the time for little girls whose parents had no flower-gardens to go around begging a bunch of lilacs, or a tulip or two. My mother always made " 'Lection cake " for us on that day. It was nothing but a

kind of sweetened bread with a shine of egg-and-
molasses on top; but we thought it delicious.

The Fourth of July and Thanksgiving Day
were the only other holidays that we made much
account of, and the former was a far more well-
behaved festival than it is in modern times. The
bells rang without stint, and at morning and
noon cannon were fired off. But torpedoes and
fire-crackers did not make the highways dangerous ; — perhaps they were thought too expensive
an amusement. Somebody delivered an oration ;
there was a good deal said about " this universal
Yankee nation " ; some rockets went up from
Salem in the evening ; we watched them from the
hill, and then went to bed, feeling that we had
been good patriots.

There was always a Fast Day, which I am
afraid most of us younger ones regarded merely
as a day when we were to eat unlimited quantities
of molasses-gingerbread, instead of sitting down
to our regular meals.

When I read about Christmas in the English
story-books, I wished we could have that beautiful holiday. But our Puritan fathers shook their
heads at Christmas.

Our Sabbath-school library books were nearly
all English reprints, and many of the story-books
were very interesting. I think that most of my
favorites were by Mrs. Sherwood. Some of them
were about life in India, — " Little Henry and

his Bearer," and "Ayah and Lady." Then there
were "The Hedge of Thorns;" "Theophilus and
Sophia;" "Anna Ross," and a whole series of
little English books that I took great delight in.

I had begun to be rather introspective and somewhat unhealthily self-critical, contrasting myself
meanwhile with my sister Lida, just a little older,
who was my usual playmate, and whom I admired
very much for what I could not help seeing, —
her unusual sweetness of disposition. I read Mrs.
Sherwood's "Infant's Progress," and I made a
personal application of it, picturing myself as the
naughty, willful "Playful," and my sister Lida
as the saintly little "Peace."

This book gave me a morbid, unhappy feeling,
while yet it had something of the fascination of
the "Pilgrim's Progress," of which it is an imita-
tion. I fancied myself followed about by a fiend-
like boy who haunted its pages, called "Inbred-
Sin;" and the story implied that there was no such
thing as getting rid of him. I began to dislike
all boys on his account. There was one who tor-
mented my sister and me — we only knew him
by name — by jumping out at us from behind
doorways or fences on our way to school, making horrid faces at us. "Inbred-Sin," I was certain, looked just like him; and the two, strangely
blended in one hideous presence, were the worst
nightmare of my dreams. There was too much
reality about that "Inbred-Sin." I felt that I

was acquainted with him. He was the hateful hero of the little allegory, as Satan is of "Paradise Lost."

I liked lessons that came to me through fables and fairy tales, although, in reading Æsop, I invariably skipped the "moral" pinned on at the end, and made one for myself, or else did without.

Mrs. Lydia Maria Child's story of "The Immortal Fountain," in the "Girl's Own Book," — which it was the joy of my heart to read, although it preached a searching sermon to me, — I applied in the same way that I did the "Infant's Progress." I thought of Lida as the gentle, unselfish Rose, and myself as the ugly Marion. She was patient and obliging, and I felt that I was the reverse. She was considered pretty, and I knew that I was the reverse of that, too. I wondered if Lida really had bathed in the Immortal Fountain, and oh, how I wished *I* could find the way there! But I feared that trying to do so would be of no use; the fairies would cross their wands to keep me back, and their wings would darken at my approach.

The book that I loved first and best, and lived upon in my childhood, was "Pilgrim's Progress." It was as a story that I cared for it, although I knew that it meant something more, — something that was already going on in my own heart and life. Oh, how I used to wish that I too could start off on a pilgrimage! It would be so much easier than the continual, discouraging struggle to be good!

The lot I most envied was that of the contented Shepherd Boy in the Valley of Humiliation, singing his cheerful songs, and wearing "the herb called *Heart's Ease* in his bosom "; but all the glorious ups and downs of the " Progress " I would gladly have shared with Christiana and her children, never desiring to turn aside into any "By-Path Meadow" while Mr. Great-Heart led the way, and the Shining Ones came down to meet us along the road. It was one of the necessities of my nature, as a child, to have some one being, real or ideal, man or woman, before whom I inwardly bowed down and worshiped. Mr. Great-Heart was the perfect hero of my imagination. Nobody, in books or out of them, compared with him. I wondered if there were really any Mr. Great-Hearts to be met with among living men.

I remember reading this beloved book once in a snow-storm, and looking up from it out among the white, wandering flakes, with a feeling that they had come down from heaven as its interpreters; that they were trying to tell me, in their airy up-and-down-flight, the story of innumerable souls. I tried to fix my eye on one particular flake, and to follow its course until it touched the earth. But I found that I could not. A little breeze was stirring, and the flake seemed to go and return, to descend and then ascend again, as if hastening homeward to the sky, losing itself at last in the airy, infinite throng, and leaving me filled with thoughts of that " great multitude, which no man could number, clothed with white robes," crowding so gloriously into the closing pages of the Bible.

Oh, if I could only be sure that I should some time be one of that invisible company! But the heavens were already beginning to look a great way off. I hummed over one of my best loved hymns, —

" Who are these in bright array ? "

and that seemed to bring them nearer again.

The history of the early martyrs, the persecutions of the Waldenses and of the Scotch Covenanters, I read and re-read with longing emulation! Why could not I be a martyr, too? It would be so beautiful to die for the truth as they did, as Jesus did! I did not understand then that He lived and died to show us what life really means, and to give us true life, like His, — the life of love to God with all our hearts, of love to all His human children for His sake ; — and that to live this life faithfully is greater even than to die a martyr's death.

It puzzled me to know what some of the talk I heard about being a Christian could mean. I saw that it was something which only men and women could comprehend. And yet they taught me to say those dear words of the Master, " Suffer the little children to come unto Me! " Surely

He meant what He said. He did not tell the children that they must receive the kingdom of God like grown people; He said that everybody must enter into it "as a little child."

But our fathers were stalwart men, with many foes to encounter. If anybody ever needed a grown-up religion, they surely did; and it became them well.

Most of our every-day reading also came to us over the sea. Miss Edgeworth's juvenile stories were in general circulation, and we knew "Harry and Lucy" and "Rosamond" almost as well as we did our own playmates. But we did not think those English children had so good a time as we did; they had to be so prim and methodical. It seemed to us that the little folks across the water never were allowed to romp and run wild; some of us may have held a vague idea that this freedom of ours was the natural inheritance of republican children only.

Primroses and cowslips and daisies bloomed in these pleasant story-books of ours, and we went a-Maying there, with our transatlantic playmates. I think we sometimes started off with our baskets, expecting to find those English flowers in our own fields. How should children be wiser than to look for every beautiful thing they have heard of, on home ground?

And, indeed, our commonest field-flowers were, many of them, importations from the mother-

country — clover, and dandelions, and ox-eye daisies. I was delighted when my mother told me
one day that a yellow flower I brought her was
a cowslip, for I thought she meant that it was the
genuine English cowslip, which I had read about.
I was disappointed to learn that it was a native
blossom, the marsh-marigold.

My sisters had some books that I appropriated
to myself a great deal: "Paul and Virginia;"
"Elizabeth, or the Exiles of Siberia;" "Nina:
an Icelandic Tale;" with the "Vicar of Wake-
field;" the "Tour to the Hebrides;" "Gulliver's
Travels;" the "Arabian Nights;" and some odd
volumes of Sir Walter Scott's novels.

I read the "Scottish Chiefs" — my first novel
— when I was about five years old. So absorbed
was I in the sorrows of Lady Helen Mar and Sir
William Wallace, that I crept into a corner where
nobody would notice me, and read on through sunset into moonlight, with eyes blurred with tears.
I did not feel that I was doing anything wrong,
for I had heard my father say he was willing his
daughters should read that one novel. He probably did not intend the remark for the ears of
his youngest, however.

My appetite for reading was omnivorous, and
I devoured a great many romances. My sisters
took them from a circulating library, many more,
perhaps, than came to my parents' knowledge;
but it was not often that one escaped me, wher-

ever it was hidden. I did not understand what I
was reading, to be sure; and that was one of the
best and worst things about it. The sentimen-
talism of some of those romances was altogether
unchildlike; but I did not take much of it in. It
was the habit of running over pages and pages to
get to the end of a story, the habit of reading
without caring what I read, that I know to have
been bad for my mind. To use a nautical expression, my brain was in danger of getting " water-
logged." There are so many more books of fic-
tion written nowadays, I do not see how the
young people who try to read one tenth of them
have any brains left for every-day use.

One result of my infantile novel-reading was
that I did not like to look at my own face in a
mirror, because it was so unlike that of heroines
always pictured with " high white foreheads " and
" cheeks of a perfect oval." Mine was round,
ruddy, and laughing with health; and, though I
practiced at the glass a good deal, I could not
lengthen it by puckering down my lips. I quite
envied the little girls who were pale and pensive-
looking, as that was the only ladyfied standard
in the romances. Of course, the chief pleasure of
reading them was that of identifying myself with
every new heroine. They began to call me a
" bookworm " at home. I did not at all relish
the title.

It was fortunate for me that I liked to be out

of doors a great deal, and that I had a brother,
John, who was willing to have me for an occasional
companion. Sometimes he would take me with
him when he went huckleberrying, up the rural
Montserrat Road, through Cat Swamp, to the edge
of Burnt Hills and Beaver Pond. He had a boy's
pride in explaining these localities to me, making
me understand that I had a guide who was familiar with every inch of the way. Then, charging
me not to move until he came back, he would
leave me sitting alone on a great craggy rock,
while he went off and filled his basket out of
sight among the bushes. Indeed, I did not want
to move, it was all so new and fascinating. The
tall pine-trees whispering to each other across the
sky - openings above me, the graceful ferns, the
velvet mosses dotted with scarlet fairy-cups, as
if the elves had just spread their table for tea,
the unspeakable charm of the spice-breathing air,
all wove a web of enchantment about me, from
which I had no wish to disentangle myself. The
silent spell of the woods held me with a power
stronger even than that of the solemn-voiced sea.

Sometimes this same brother would get permission to take me on a longer excursion, — to
visit the old homestead at " The Farms." Three
or four miles was not thought too long a walk
for a healthy child of five years ; and that road,
in the old time, led through a rural Paradise,
beautiful at every season, — whether it were the

time of song-sparrows and violets, of wild roses, of coral-hung barberry-bushes, or of fallen leaves and snow-drifts. The wildness of the road, now exchanged for elegant modern cultivation, was its great charm to us. We stopped at the Cove Brook to hear the cat-birds sing, and at Mingo's Beach to revel in the sudden surprise of the open sea, and to listen to the chant of the waves, always stronger and grander there than anywhere along the shore. We passed under dark wooded cliffs out into sunny openings, the last of which held under its skirting pines the secret of the prettiest woodpath to us in all the world, the path to the ancestral farm-house.

We found children enough to play with there, — as numerous a family as our own. We were sometimes, I fancy, the added drop too much of already overflowing juvenility. Farther down the road, where the cousins were all grown-up men and women, Aunt Betsey's cordial, old-fashioned hospitality sometimes detained us a day or two. We watched the milking, and fed the chickens, and fared gloriously. Aunt Betsey could not have done more to entertain us, had we been the President's children.

I have always cherished the memory of a certain pair of large-bowed spectacles that she wore, and of the green calash, held by a ribbon bridle, that sheltered her head, when she walked up from the shore to see us, as she often did. They an-

nounced to us the approach of inexhaustible kind-
liness and good cheer. We took in a home-feeling
with the words " Aunt Betsey " then and always.
She had just the husband that belonged to her
in my Uncle David, an upright man, frank-faced,
large - hearted, and spiritually minded. He was
my father's favorite brother, and to our branch
of the family " The Farms " meant " Uncle David
and Aunt Betsey."

My brother John's plans for my entertainment
did not always harmonize entirely with my own
ideas. He had an inventive mind, and wanted
me to share his boyish sports. But I did not
like to ride in a wheelbarrow, nor to walk on
stilts, nor even to coast down the hill on his sled
and I always got a tumble, if I tried, for I was
rather a clumsy child ; besides, I much preferred
girls' quieter games.

We were seldom permitted to play with any
boys except our brothers. I drew the inference
that our boys must be a great deal better than
" the other boys." My brother John had some
fine play-fellows, but he seemed to consider me in
the way when they were his guests. Occasionally
we would forget that the neighbor-boys were not
girls, and would find ourselves all playing together in delightful unconsciousness; although
possibly a thought, like that of the " Ettrick
Shepherd," may now and then have flitted through
the mind of some masculine juvenile: —

"Why the boys should drive away
Little sweet maidens from the play,
Or love to banter and fight so well, —
That 's the thing I never could tell."

One day I thoughtlessly accepted an invitation
to get through a gap in the garden-fence, to
where the doctor's two boys were preparing to
take an imaginary sleigh - ride in midsummer.
The sleigh was stranded among tall weeds and
cornstalks, but I was politely handed in by the
elder boy, who sat down by my side and tucked
his little brother in front at our feet, informing
me that we were father and mother and little son,
going to take a ride to Newburyport. He had
found an old pair of reins and tied them to a saw-
horse, that he switched and " Gee-up "-ed vigor-
ously. The journey was as brief as delightful.
I ran home feeling like the heroine of an elope-
ment, asking myself meanwhile, " What would
my brother John say if he knew I had been playing with boys?" He was very particular about
his sisters' behavior. But I incautiously said to
one sister in whom I did not usually confide, that
I thought James was the nicest boy in the lane,
and that I liked his little brother Charles, too.
She laughed at me so unmercifully for making
the remark, that I never dared look towards the
gap in the fence again, beyond which I could hear
the boys' voices around the old sleigh where they
were playing, entirely forgetful of their former

traveling companion. Still, I continued to think
that my courteous cavalier, James, *was* the nicest
boy in the lane.

My brother's vigilant care of his two youngest
sisters was once the occasion to them of a serious
fright. My grandfather — the sexton — sometimes trusted him to toll the bell for a funeral. In
those days the bell was tolled for everybody who
died. John was social, and did not like to go up
into the belfry and stay an hour or so alone, and
as my grandfather positively forbade him to take
any other boy up there, he one day got permission for us two little girls to go with him, for
company. We had to climb up a great many
stairs, and the last flight was inclosed by a rough
door with a lock inside, which he was charged to
fasten, so that no mischievous boys should follow.

It was strange to be standing up there in the
air, gazing over the balcony-railing down into the
street, where the men and women looked so small,
and across to the water and the ships in the east,
and the clouds and hills in the west! But when
he struck the tongue against the great bell, close
to our ears, it was more than we were prepared
for. The little sister, scarcely three years old,
screamed and shrieked, —

" I shall be stunned-ded! I shall be stunned-
ded!" I do not know where she had picked up
that final syllable, but it made her terror much
more emphatic. Still the great waves of solemn

sound went eddying on, over the hills and over the sea, and we had to hear it all, though we stopped our ears with our fingers.   It was an immense relief to us when the last stroke of the passing-bell was struck, and John said we could go down.

He took the key from his pocket and was fitting it into the lock, when it slipped, dropping down through a wide crack in the floor, beyond our reach.   Now the little sister cried again, and would not be pacified ; and when I looked up and caught John's blank, dismayed look, I began to feel like crying, too.   The question went swiftly through my mind, — How many days can we stay up here without starving to death ? — for I really thought we should never get down out of our prison in the air : never see our mother's face again.

But my brother's wits returned to him.   He led us back to the balcony, and shouted over the railing to a boy in the street, making him understand that he must go and inform my father that we were locked into the belfry.   It was not long before we saw both him and my grandfather on their way to the church.   They came up to the little door, and told us to push with our united strength against it.   The rusty lock soon yielded, and how good it was to look into those two beloved human faces once more !   But we little girls were not invited to join my brother again when he tolled the bell : if we had been, I think we should have promptly declined the invitation.

Many of my childish misadventures came to me in connection with my little sister, who, having been much indulged, took it for granted that she could always have what she wanted.

One day we two were allowed to take a walk together; I, as the older, being supposed to take care of her. Although we were only going towards the Cove, over a secluded road, she insisted upon wearing a brand-new pair of red morocco boots. All went well until we came to a bog by the roadside, where sweet-flag and cat-tails grew. Out in the middle of the bog, where no venturesome boy had ever attempted their seizure, there were many tall, fine-looking brown cat-tails growing. She caught sight of them, and before I saw what she was doing, she had shot from my side like an arrow from the bow, and was far out on the black, quaking surface, that at first upheld her light weight. I stood petrified with horror. I knew all about that dangerous place. I had been told that nobody had ever found out how deep that mud was. I had uttered just one imploring "Come back!" when she turned to me with a shriek, throwing up her arms towards me. She was sinking! There was nobody in sight, and there was no time to think. I ran, or rather flew, across the bog, with just one thought in my mind, "I have *got* to get her out!" Some angel must

have prevented me from making a misstep, and
sinking with her.   I felt the power of a giant
suddenly taking possession of my small frame.
Quicker than I could tell of it, I had given one
tremendous pull (she had already sunk above her
boot-tops), and had dragged her back to the road.
It is a marvel to me now how I — a child of
scarcely six years — succeeded in rescuing her.   It
did not seem to me as if I were doing it myself,
but as if some unseen Power had taken possession
of me for a moment, and made me do it.   And I
suppose that when we act from a sudden impulse
to help another out of trouble, it never is ourself
that does the good deed.   The Highest Strength
just takes us and uses us.   I certainly felt equal
to going straight through the earth to China after
my little sister, if she had sunk out of sight.

We were two miserable looking children when
we reached home, the sticky ooze having changed
her feet into unmanageable lumps of mud, with
which my own clothes also were soiled.   I had to
drag or carry her all the way, for she could not
or would not walk a step.   And alas for the morocco boots!   They were never again *red*.   I also
received a scolding for not taking better care of
my little sister, and I was not very soon allowed
again to have her company in my rambles.

We usually joined with other little neighbor
girls in some out-of-door amusement near home.
And our sports, as well as our books, had a spice

of Merry Old England. They were full of kings
and queens, and made sharp contrasts, as well as
odd mixtures, with the homeliness of our every-
day life.

One of them, a sort of rhymed dialogue, began
with the couplet : —

> " Queen Anne, Queen Anne, she sits in the sun,
> As fair as a lady, as white as a nun."

If " Queen Anne " did not give a right guess as
to which hand of the messenger held the king's
letter to her, she was contemptuously informed
that she was

> " as brown as a bun."

In another game, four little girls joined hands
across, in couples, chanting : —

> " I wish my father were a king,
> I wish my mother were a queen,
> And I a little companion ! "

concluding with a close embrace in a dizzying
whirl, breathlessly shouting all together, —

> " A bundle of fagots ! A bundle of fagots ! "

In a third, which may have begun with a juvenile reacting of the Colonial struggle for liberty,
we ranged ourselves under two leaders, who made
an archway over our heads of their lifted hands
and arms, saying, as we passed beneath, —

> " Lift up the gates as high as the sky,
> And let King George and his army pass by ! "

We were told to whisper " Oranges " or

" Lemons " for a pass-word ; and " Oranges " always won the larger enlistment, whether British
or American.

And then there was " Grandmother Gray," and
the
> " Old woman from Newfoundland,
> With all her children in her hand ; "

and the
> " Knight from Spain
> Inquiring for your daughter Jane,"

and numberless others, nearly all of them bearing
a distinct Old World flavor.

One of our play-places was an unoccupied end
of the burying-ground, overhung by the Colonel's
apple-trees and close under his wall, so that we
should not be too near the grave-stones.

I do not think that death was at all a real thing
to me or to my brothers and sisters at this time.
We lived so near the grave-yard that it seemed
merely the extension of our garden. We wandered there at will, trying to decipher the moss-
grown inscriptions, and wondering at the homely
carvings of cross-bones and cherubs and willow-
trees on the gray slate-stones. I did not associate
those long green mounds with people who had once
lived, though we were careful, having been so instructed, not to step on the graves. To ramble
about there and puzzle ourselves with the names
and dates, was like turning over the pages of a
curious old book. We had not the least feeling of
irreverence in taking the edge of the grave-yard

for our playground. It was known as "the old burying-ground"; and we children regarded it with a sort of affectionate freedom, as we would a grandmother, *because* it was old.

That, indeed, was one peculiar attraction of the town itself; it was old, and it seemed old, much older than it does now. There was only one main street, said to have been the first settlers' cowpath to Wenham, which might account for its zigzag picturesqueness. All the rest were courts or lanes.

The town used to wear a delightful air of drowsiness, as if she had stretched herself out for an afternoon nap, with her head towards her old mother, Salem, and her whole length reclining towards the sea, till she felt at her feet, through her green robes, the dip of the deep water at the Farms. All her elder children recognized in her quiet steady-going ways a maternal unity and strength of character, as of a town that under-stood her own plans, and had settled down to peaceful, permanent habits.

Her spirit was that of most of our Massachu-setts coast-towns. They were transplanted shoots of Old England. And it was the voice of a mother-country more ancient than their own, that little children heard crooning across the sea in their cradle-hymns and nursery-songs.

VI.

OUR close relationship to Old England was sometimes a little misleading to us juveniles. The conditions of our life were entirely different, but we read her descriptive stories and sang her songs as if they were true for us, too. One of the first things I learned to repeat — I think it was in the spelling-book — began with the verse : —

> "I thank the goodness and the grace
> That on my birth has smiled,
> And made me, in these latter days,
> A happy *English* child."

And some lines of a very familiar hymn by Dr. Watts ran thus : —

> "Whene'er I take my walks abroad,
> How many poor I see.
> . . . .
> "How many children in the street
> Half naked I behold ;
> While I am clothed from head to feet,
> And sheltered from the cold."

Now a ragged, half-clothed child, or one that could really be called poor, in the extreme sense of the word, was the rarest of all sights in a thrifty New England town fifty years ago. I used to look sharply for those children, but I never could see

one. And a beggár! Oh, if a real beggar would
come along, like the one described in

"Pity the sorrows of a poor old man,"

what a wonderful event that would be! I believe
I had more curiosity about a beggar, and more
ignorance, too, than about a king. The poem
read : —

"A pampered menial drove me from the door."

What sort of creature could a "pampered menial" be? Nothing that had ever come under our
observation corresponded to the words. Nor was
it easy for us to attach any meaning to the word
"servant." There were women who came in occasionally to do the washing, or to help about extra
work. But they were decently clothed, and had
homes of their own, more or less comfortable, and
their quaint talk and free - and - easy ways were
often as much of a lift to the household as the
actual assistance they rendered.

I settled down upon the conclusion that "rich"
and "poor" were book - words only, describing
something far off, and having nothing to do with
our every-day experience. My mental definition
of "rich people," from home observation, was
something like this : People who live in three-
story houses, and keep their green blinds closed,
and hardly ever come out and talk with the folks
in the street. There were a few such houses in
Beverly, and a great many in Salem, where my

mother sometimes took me for a shopping walk. But I did not suppose that any of the people who lived near us were *very* rich, like those in books.

Everybody about us worked, and we expected to take hold of our part while young. I think we were rather eager to begin, for we believed that work would make men and women of us.

I, however, was not naturally an industrious child, but quite the reverse. When my father sent us down to weed his vegetable-garden at the foot of the lane, I, the youngest of his weeders, liked to go with the rest, but not for the sake of the work or the pay. I generally gave it up before I had weeded half a bed. It made me so warm! and my back did ache so! I stole off into the shade of the great apple-trees, and let the west wind fan my hot cheeks, and looked up into the boughs, and listened to the many, many birds that seemed chattering to each other in a language of their own. What was it they were saying? and why could not I understand it? Perhaps I should, sometime. I had read of people who did, in fairy tales.

When the others started homeward, I followed. I did not mind their calling me lazy, nor that my father gave me only one tarnished copper cent, while Lida received two or three bright ones. I had had what I wanted most. I would rather sit under the apple-trees and hear the birds sing than have a whole handful of bright copper pen-

nies. It was well for my father and his garden
that his other children were not like me.

The work which I was born to, but had not begun to do, was sometimes a serious weight upon
my small, forecasting brain.

One of my hymns ended with the lines, —

> "With books, and work, and healthful play,
>   May my first years be passed,
> That I may give, for every day,
>   Some good account at last."

I knew all about the books and the play; but
the work, — how should I ever learn to do it?

My father had always strongly emphasized his
wish that all his children, girls as well as boys,
should have some independent means of self-support by the labor of their hands; that every one
should, as was the general custom, "learn a trade."
Tailor's work — the finishing of men's outside
garments — was the "trade" learned most frequently by women in those days, and one or more
of my older sisters worked at it; I think it must
have been at home, for I somehow or somewhere
got the idea, while I was a small child, that the
chief end of woman was to make clothing for
mankind.

This thought came over me with a sudden
dread one Sabbath morning when I was a tod-
dling thing, led along by my sister, behind my
father and mother. As they walked arm in arm
before me, I lifted my eyes from my father's heels

to his head, and mused : "How tall he is! and
how long his coat looks! and how many thousand,
thousand stitches there must be in his coat and
pantaloons! And I suppose I have got to grow
up and have a husband, and put all those little
stitches into *his* coats and pantaloons. Oh, I
never, never can do it!" A shiver of utter discouragement went through me. With that task
before me, it hardly seemed to me as if life were
worth living. I went on to meeting, and I suppose I forgot my trouble in a hymn, but for the
moment it was real. It was not the only time in
my life that I have tired myself out with crossing
bridges to which I never came.

Another trial confronted me in the shape of an
ideal but impossible patchwork quilt. We learned
to sew patchwork at school, while we were learning the alphabet; and almost every girl, large or
small, had a bed-quilt of her own begun, with an
eye to future house furnishing. I was not over
fond of sewing, but I thought it best to begin
mine early.

So I collected a few squares of calico, and undertook to put them together in my usual independent way, without asking direction. I liked as-
sorting those little figured bits of cotton cloth, for
they were scraps of gowns I had seen worn, and
they reminded me of the persons who wore them.
One fragment, in particular, was like a picture to
me. It was a delicate pink and brown sea-moss

pattern, on a white ground, a piece of a dress belonging to my married sister, who was to me bride
and angel in one. I always saw her face before
me when I unfolded this scrap, — a face with an
expression truly heavenly in its loveliness. Heaven
claimed her before my childhood was ended. Her
beautiful form was laid to rest in mid-ocean, too
deep to be pillowed among the soft sea-mosses.
But she lived long enough to make a heaven of
my childhood whenever she came home.

One of the sweetest of our familiar hymns I
always think of as belonging to her, and as a still
unbroken bond between her spirit and mine. She
had come back to us for a brief visit, soon after
her marriage, with some deep, new experience of
spiritual realities which I, a child of four or five
years, felt in the very tones of her voice, and in
the expression of her eyes.

My mother told her of my fondness for the
hymn-book, and she turned to me with a smile
and said, " Won't you learn one hymn for me —
one hymn that I love very much ? "

Would I not? She could not guess how happy
she made me by wishing me to do anything for
her sake. The hymn was, —

" Whilst Thee I seek, protecting Power."

In a few minutes I repeated the whole to her ;
and its own beauty, pervaded with the tenderness of her love for me, fixed it at once indelibly

in my memory. Perhaps I shall repeat it to her again, deepened with a lifetime's meaning, beyond the sea, and beyond the stars.

I could dream over my patchwork, but I could not bring it into conventional shape. My sisters, whose fingers had been educated, called my sewing "gobblings." I grew disgusted with it myself, and gave away all my pieces except the pretty sea-moss pattern, which I was not willing to see patched up with common calico. It was evident that I should never conquer fate with my needle.

Among other domestic traditions of the old times was the saying that every girl must have a pillow-case full of stockings of her own knitting before she was married. Here was another mountain before me, for I took it for granted that marrying was inevitable — one of the things that everybody must do, like learning to read, or going to meeting.

I began to knit my own stockings when I was six or seven years old, and kept on, until home-made stockings went out of fashion. The pillow-case full, however, was never attempted, any more than the patchwork quilt. I heard somebody say one day that there must always be one "old maid" in every family of girls, and I accepted the prophecy of some of my elders, that I was to be that one. I was rather glad to know that freedom of choice in the matter was possible.

One day, when we younger ones were hanging

about my golden-haired and golden-hearted sister Emilie, teasing her with wondering questions about our future, she announced to us (she had reached the mature age of fifteen years) that she intended to be an old maid, and that we might all come and live with her. Some one listening reproved her, but she said, " Why, if they fit themselves to be good, helpful, cheerful old maids, they will certainly be better wives, if they ever are married," and that maxim I laid by in my memory for future contingencies, for I believed in every word she ever uttered. She herself, however, did not carry out her girlish intention. " Her children arise up and call her blessed ; her husband also ; and he praiseth her." But the little sisters she used to fondle as her " babies " have never allowed their own years nor her changed relations to cancel their claim upon her motherly sympathies.

I regard it as a great privilege to have been one of a large family, and nearly the youngest. We had strong family resemblances, and yet no two seemed at all alike. It was like rehearsing in a small world each our own part in the great one awaiting us. If we little ones occasionally had some severe snubbing mixed with the petting and praising and loving, that was wholesome for us, and not at all to be regretted.

Almost every one of my sisters had some distinctive aptitude with her fingers. One worked

exquisite lace-embroidery; another had a knack
at cutting and fitting her doll's clothing so perfectly that the wooden lady was always a typical
specimen of the genteel doll-world; and another
was an expert at fine stitching, so delicately done
that it was a pleasure to see or to wear anything
her needle had touched. I had none of these
gifts. I looked on and admired, and sometimes
tried to imitate, but my efforts usually ended in
defeat and mortification.

I did like to knit, however, and I could shape
a stocking tolerably well. My fondness for this
kind of work was chiefly because it did not require much thought. Except when there was
" widening " or " narrowing " to be done, I did not
need to keep my eyes upon it at all. So I took
a book upon my lap and read, and read, while
the needles clicked on, comforting me with the
reminder that I was not absolutely unemployed,
while yet I was having a good time reading.

I began to know that I liked poetry, and to
think a good deal about it at my childish work.
Outside of the hymn-book, the first rhymes I
committed to memory were in the " Old Farmer's
Almanac," files of which hung in the chimney
corner, and were an inexhaustible source of entertainment to us younger ones.

My father kept his newspapers also carefully
filed away in the garret, but we made sad havoc
among the " Palladiums " and other journals that

we ought to have kept as antiquarian treasures. We valued the anecdote column and the poet's corner only ; these we clipped unsparingly for our scrap-books.

A tattered copy of Johnson's large Dictionary was a great delight to me, on account of the specimens of English versification which I found in the Introduction. I learned them as if they were so many poems. I used to keep this old volume close to my pillow ; and I amused myself when I awoke in the morning by reciting its jingling contrasts of iambic and trochaic and dactylic metre, and thinking what a charming occupation it must be to " make up " verses.

I made my first rhymes when I was about seven years old. My brother John proposed " writing poetry " as a rainy-day amusement, one afternoon when we two were sent up into the garret to entertain ourselves without disturbing the family. He soon grew tired of his unavailing attempts, but I produced two stanzas, the first of which read thus : —

> One summer day, said little Jane,
> We were walking down a shady lane,
> When suddenly the wind blew high,
> And the red lightning flashed in the sky.

The second stanza descended in a dreadfully abrupt anti-climax ; but I was blissfully ignorant of rhetoricians' rules, and supposed that the rhyme

was the only important thing. It may amuse **my**
child-readers if I give them this verse too: —

> The peals of thunder, how they rolled!
> *And I felt myself a little cooled;*
> *For I before had been quite warm;*
> But now around me was a storm.

My brother was surprised at my success, and I
believe I thought my verses quite fine, too. But
I was rather sorry that I had written them, for I
had to say them over to the family, and then
they sounded silly. The habit was formed, however, and I went on writing little books of ballads,
which I illustrated with colors from my toy paint-
box, and then squeezed down into the cracks of
the garret floor, for fear that somebody would
find them.

My fame crept out among the neighbors, nevertheless. I was even invited to write some verses
in a young lady's album; and Aunt Hannah
asked me to repeat my verses to her. I considered myself greatly honored by both requests.

My fondness for books began very early. At
the age of four I had formed the plan of col-
lecting a library. Not of limp, paper-covered
picture-books, such as people give to babies; no!
I wanted books with stiff covers, that could stand
up side by side on a shelf, and maintain their
own character as books. But I did not know
how to make a beginning, for mine were all of
the kind manufactured for infancy, and I thought

they deserved no better fate than to be tossed about among my rag-babies and playthings.

One day, however, I found among some rubbish in a corner a volume with one good stiff cover; the other was missing. It did not look so very old, nor as if it had been much read; neither did it look very inviting to me as I turned its leaves. On its title-page I read : " The Life of John Calvin." I did not know who he was, but a book was a book to me, and this would do as well as any to begin my library with. I looked upon it as a treasure, and to make sure of my claim, I took it down to my mother and timidly asked if I might have it for my own. She gave me in reply a rather amused " Yes," and I ran back happy, and began my library by setting John Calvin upright on a beam under the garret eaves, my " make-believe " book-case shelf.

I was proud of my literary property, and filled out the shelf in fancy with a row of books, every one of which should have two stiff covers. But I found no more neglected volumes that I could adopt. John Calvin was left to a lonely fate, and I am afraid that at last the mice devoured him. Before I had quite forgotten him, however, I did pick up one other book of about his size, and in the same one-covered condition; and this attracted me more, because it was in verse. Rhyme had always a sort of magnetic power over me, whether I caught at any idea it contained or not.

This was written in the measure which I afterwards learned was called Spenserian.   It was
Byron's "Vision of Judgment," and Southey's
also was bound up with it.

Southey's hexameters were too much of a
mouthful for me, but Byron's lines jingled, and
apparently told a story about something.   St. Peter came into it, and King George the Third; neither of which names meant anything to me ; but
the scenery seemed to be somewhere up among
the clouds, and I, unsuspicious of the author's irreverence, took it for a sort of semi-Biblical fairy
tale.

There was on my mother's bed a covering of
pink chintz, pictured all over with the figure of a
man sitting on a cloud, holding a bunch of keys.
I put the two together in my mind, imagining the
chintz counterpane to be an illustration of the
poem, or the poem an explanation of the counterpane.   For the stanza I liked best began with the
words, —

> " St. Peter sat at the celestial gate,
> And nodded o'er his keys."

I invented a pronunciation for the long words, and
went about the house reciting grandly, —

> " St. Peter sat at the *kelestikal* gate,
> And nodded o'er his keys."

That volume, swept back to me with the rubbish of Time, still reminds me, forlorn and half-

clad, of my childish fondness for its mock-magnificence.

John Calvin and Lord Byron were rather a peculiar combination, as the foundation of an infant's library; but I was not aware of any unfitness or incompatibility. To me they were two brother-books, like each other in their refusal to wear limp covers.

It is amusing to recall the rapid succession of contrasts in one child's tastes. I felt no incongruity between Dr. Watts and Mother Goose. I supplemented " Pibroch of Donuil Dhu " and

"Lochiel, Lochiel, beware of the day,"

with "Yankee Doodle " and the " Diverting History of John Gilpin; " and with the glamour of some fairy tale I had just read still haunting me, I would run out of doors eating a big piece of bread and butter, — sweeter than any has tasted since, — and would jump up towards the crows cawing high above me, cawing back to them, and half wishing I too were a crow to make the sky ring with my glee.

After Dr. Watts's hymns the first poetry I took great delight in greeted me upon the pages of the " American First Class Book," handed down from older pupils in the little private school which my sisters and I attended when Aunt Hannah had done all she could for us. That book was a collection of excellent literary extracts, made by

one who was himself an author and a poet. It
deserved to be called "first-class" in another
sense than that which was understood by its title.
I cannot think that modern reading books have
improved upon it much. It contained poems from
Wordsworth, passages from Shakespeare's plays,
among them the pathetic dialogue between Hu-
bert and little Prince Arthur, whose appeal to
have his eyes spared, brought many a tear to my
own. Bryant's "Waterfowl" and "Thanatopsis"
were there also; and Neal's, —

> "There's a fierce gray bird with a bending beak,"

that the boys loved so dearly to "declaim;" and
another poem by this last author, which we all
liked to read, partly from a childish love of the
tragic, and partly for its graphic description of
an avalanche's movement: —

> "Slowly it came in its mountain wrath,
> And the forests vanished before its path;
> And the rude cliffs bowed; and the waters fled, —
> And the valley of life was the tomb of the dead."

In reading this "Swiss Minstrel's Lament over
the Ruins of Goldau," I first felt my imagination
thrilled with the terrible beauty of the mountains
— a terror and a sublimity which attracted my
thoughts far more than it awed them. But the
poem in which they burst upon me as real pres-
ences, unseen, yet known in their remote splendor
as kingly friends before whom I could bow, yet

with whom I could aspire, — for something like this
I think mountains must always be to those who
truly love them, — was Coleridge's " Mont Blanc
before Sunrise," in this same " First Class Book."
I believe that poetry really first took possession of
me in that poem, so that afterwards I could not
easily mistake the genuineness of its ring, though
my ear might not be sufficiently trained to catch
its subtler harmonies. This great mountain poem
struck some hidden key-note in my nature, and I
knew thenceforth something of what it was to live
in poetry, and to have it live in me. Of course
I did not consider my own foolish little versifying poetry. The child of eight or nine years regarded her rhymes as only one among her many
games and pastimes.

But with this ideal picture of mountain scenery
there came to me a revelation of poetry as the one
unattainable something which I must reach out
after, because I could not live without it. The
thought of it was to me like the thought of God
and of truth. To leave out poetry would be to
lose the real meaning of life. I felt this very
blindly and vaguely, no doubt; but the feeling was
deep. It was as if Mont Blanc stood visibly before me, while I murmured to myself in lonely
places —

"Motionless torrents! silent cataracts!
Who made you glorious as the gates of heaven
Beneath the keen full moon ?   Who bade the sun
Clothe you with rainbows ?   Who with lovely flowers
Of living blue spread garlands at your feet ? "

And then the

"Pine groves with their soft and soul-like sound"

gave glorious answer, with the streams and torrents, and my child-heart in its trance echoed the
poet's invocation, —

"Rise, like a cloud of incense from the earth!
And tell the stars, and tell the rising sun,
Earth, with her thousand voices, calls on GOD!"

I have never visited Switzerland, but I surely
saw the Alps, with Coleridge, in my childhood.
And although I never stood face to face with
mountains until I was a mature woman, always,
after this vision of them, they were blended with
my dream of whatever is pure and lofty in human possibilities, — like a white ideal beckoning
me on.

Since I am writing these recollections for the
young, I may say here that I regard a love for
poetry as one of the most needful and helpful
elements in the life-outfit of a human being. It
was the greatest of blessings to me, in the long
days of toil to which I was shut in much earlier
than most young girls are, that the poetry I held
in my memory breathed its enchanted atmosphere
through me and around me, and touched even dull
drudgery with its sunshine.

Hard work, however, has its own illumination
— if done as duty — which worldliness has not;
and worldliness seems to be the greatest tempta-

tion and danger of young people in this generation. Poetry is one of the angels whose presence will drive out this sordid demon, if anything less than the Power of the Highest can. But poetry *is* of the Highest. It is the Divine Voice, always, that we recognize through the poet's, whenever he most deeply moves our souls.

Reason and observation, as well as my own experience, assure me also that it is *great* poetry — even the greatest — which the youngest crave, and upon which they may be fed, because it is the simplest. Nature does not write down her sunsets, her starry skies, her mountains, and her oceans in some smaller style, to suit the comprehension of little children ; they do not need any such dilution.

So I go back to the "American First Class Book," and affirm it to have been one of the best of reading-books, because it gave us children a taste of the finest poetry and prose which had been written in our English tongue, by British and by American authors. Among the pieces which left a permanent impression upon my mind I recall Wirt's description of the eloquent blind preacher to whom he listened in the forest wilderness of the Blue Ridge, a remarkable word-portrait, in which the very tones of the sightless speaker's voice seemed to be reproduced. I believe that the first words I ever remembered of any sermon were those contained in the grand, brief sentence, — " Socrates died like a philosopher ; but Jesus Christ — like a God ! "

Very vivid, too, is the recollection of the exquisite little prose idyl of " Moss-Side," from " Lights and Shadows of Scottish Life."

From the few short words with which it began — " Gilbert Ainslee was a poor man, and he had been a poor man all the days of his life " — to the happy waking of his little daughter Margaret out of her fever-sleep with which it ended, it was one sweet picture of lowly life and honorable poverty irradiated with sacred home-affections, and cheerful in its rustic homeliness as the blossoms and wild birds of the moorland and the magic touch of Christopher North could make it. I thought as I read, —

" How much pleasanter it must be to be poor than to be rich — at least in Scotland ! "

For I was beginning to be made aware that poverty was a possible visitation to our own household ; and that, in our Cape Ann corner of Massachusetts, we might find it neither comfortable nor picturesque. After my father's death, our way of living, never luxurious, grew more and more frugal. Now and then I heard mysterious allusions to " the wolf at the door " ; and it was whispered that, to escape him, we might all have to turn our backs upon the home where we were born, and find our safety in the busy world, working among strangers for our daily bread. Before I had reached my tenth year I began to have rather disturbed dreams of what it might soon mean for me to " earn my own living."

VII.

A CHILD does not easily comprehend even the plain fact of death. Though I had looked upon my father's still, pale face in his coffin, the impression it left upon me was of sleep; more peaceful and sacred than common slumber, yet only sleep. My dreams of him were for a long time so vivid that I would say to myself, " He was here yesterday; he will be here again to-morrow," with a feeling that amounted to expectation.

We missed him, we children large and small who made up the yet untrained home crew, as a ship misses the man at the helm. His grave, clear perception of what was best for us, his brief words that decided, once for all, the course we were to take, had been far more to us than we knew.

It was hardest of all for my mother, who had been accustomed to depend entirely upon him. Left with her eight children, the eldest a boy of eighteen years, and with no property except the roof that sheltered us and a small strip of land, her situation was full of perplexities which we little ones could not at all understand. To be fed like the ravens and clothed like the grass of the field seemed to me, for one, a perfectly natural thing, and I often wondered why my mother was so fretted and anxious.

I knew that she believed in God, and in the promises of the Bible, and yet she seemed sometimes to forget everything but her troubles and her helplessness. I felt almost like preaching to her, but I was too small a child to do that, I well knew; so I did the next best thing I could think of — I sang hymns as if singing to myself, while I meant them for her. Sitting at the window with my book and my knitting, while she was preparing dinner or supper with a depressed air because she missed the abundant provision to which she had been accustomed, I would go from hymn to hymn, selecting those which I thought would be most comforting to her, out of the many that my memory-book contained, and taking care to pronounce the words distinctly.

I was glad to observe that she listened to

"Come, ye disconsolate,"

and

"How firm a foundation;"

and that she grew more cheerful; though I did not feel sure that my singing cheered her so much as some happier thought that had come to her out of her own heart. Nobody but my mother, indeed, would have called my chirping singing. But as she did not seem displeased, I went on,

a little more confidently, with some hymns that I
loved for their starry suggestions, —

> "When marshaled on the nightly plain,"

and

> "Brightest and best of the sons of the morning,"

and

> "Watchman, tell us of the night?"

The most beautiful picture in the Bible to me,
certainly the loveliest in the Old Testament, had
always been that one painted by prophecy, of the
time when wild and tame creatures should live together in peace, and children should be their fearless playmates. Even the savage wolf Poverty
would be pleasant and neighborly then, no doubt!
A Little Child among them, leading them, stood
looking wistfully down through the soft sunrise
of that approaching day, into the cold and darkness of the world. Oh, it would be so much better than the garden of Eden!

Yes, and it would be a great deal better, I
thought, to live in the millennium, than even to
die and go to heaven, although so many people
around me talked as if that were the most desirable thing of all. But I could never understand
why, if God sent us here, we should be in haste
to get away, even to go to a pleasanter place.

I was perplexed by a good many matters besides. I had learned to keep most of my thoughts
to myself, but I did venture to ask about the Res-
surrection — how it was that those who had died
and gone straight to heaven, and had been sing-

ing there for thousands of years, could have any use for the dust to which their bodies had returned. Were they not already as alive as they could be? I found that there were different ideas of the resurrection among "orthodox" people, even then. I was told however, that this was too deep a matter for me, and so I ceased asking questions. But I pondered the matter of death; what did it mean? The Apostle Paul gave me more light on the subject than any of the ministers did. And, as usual, a poem helped me. It was Pope's Ode, beginning with, —

> "Vital spark of heavenly flame," —

which I learned out of a reading-book. To die was to "languish into life." That was the meaning of it! and I loved to repeat to myself the words, —

> "Hark! they whisper: angels say,
> 'Sister spirit, come away!' —
> . . . .
> The world recedes; it disappears!
> Heaven opens on my eyes! my ears
> With sounds seraphic ring."

A hymn that I learned a little later expressed to me the same satisfying thought: —

> "For strangers into life we come,
> And dying is but going home."

The Apostle's words, with which the song of "The Dying Christian to his Soul" ends, left the whole cloudy question lit up with sunshine, to my childish thoughts: —

" O grave, where is thy victory ?
  O death, where is thy sting ? "

My father was dead ; but that only meant that
he had gone to a better home than the one he
lived in with us, and by and by we should go
home, too.

Meanwhile the millennium was coming, and
some people thought it was very near. And what
was the millennium ? Why, the time when everybody on earth would live just as they do in
heaven. Nobody would be selfish, nobody would
be unkind; no! not so much as in a single
thought. What a delightful world this would be
to live in then ! Heaven itself could scarcely be
much better! Perhaps people would not die at
all, but, when the right time came, would slip
quietly away into heaven, just as Enoch did.

My father had believed in the near millennium.
His very last writing, in his sick-room, was a
penciled computation, from the prophets, of the
time when it would begin. The first minister
who preached in our church, long before I was
born, had studied the subject much, and had written books upon this, his favorite theme. The
thought of it was continually breaking out, like
bloom and sunshine, from the stern doctrines of
the period.

One question in this connection puzzled me a
good deal. Were people going to be made good
in spite of themselves, whether they wanted to or

not? And what would be done with the bad ones,
if there were any left? I did not like to think
of their being killed off, and yet everybody must
be good, or it would not be a true millennium.

It certainly would not matter much who was
rich, and who was poor, if goodness, and not
money, was the thing everybody cared for. Oh, if
the millennium would only begin now! I felt as
if it were hardly fair to me that I should not be
here during those happy thousand years, when I
wanted to so much. But I had not lived even my
short life in the world without learning something of my own faults and perversities; and
when I saw that there was no sign of an approaching millennium in my heart I had to conclude
that it might be a great way off, after all. Yet
the very thought of it brought warmth and illumination to my dreams by day and by night. It
was coming, some time! And the people who
were in heaven would be as glad of it as those
who remained on earth.

That it was a hard world for my mother and
her children to live in at present I could not help
seeing. The older members of the family found
occupations by which the domestic burdens were
lifted a little; but, with only the three youngest to
clothe and to keep at school, there was still much
more outgo than income, and my mother's discouragement every day increased.

My eldest brother had gone to sea with a relative who was master of a merchant vessel in the South American trade. His inclination led him that way; it seemed to open before him a prospect of profitable business, and my mother looked upon him as her future stay and support.

One day she came in among us children looking strangely excited. I heard her tell some one afterwards that she had just been to hear Father Taylor preach, the sailors' minister, whose coming to our town must have been a rare occurrence. His words had touched her personally, for he had spoken to mothers whose first-born had left them to venture upon strange seas and to seek unknown lands. He had even given to the wanderer he described the name of her own absent son — "Benjamin." As she left the church she met a neighbor who informed her that the brig "Mexican" had arrived at Salem, in trouble. It was the vessel in which my brother had sailed only a short time before, expecting to be absent for months. "Pirates" was the only word we children caught, as she hastened away from the house, not knowing whether her son was alive or not. Fortunately, the news hardly reached the town before my brother himself did. She met him in the street, and brought him home with her, forgetting all her anxieties in her joy at his safety.

The "Mexican" had been attacked on the high seas by the piratical craft "Panda," robbed of twenty thousand dollars in specie, set on fire, and abandoned to her fate, with the crew fastened down in the hold. One small skylight had accidentally been overlooked by the freebooters. The captain discovered it, and making his way through it to the deck, succeeded in putting out the fire, else vessel and sailors would have sunk together, and their fate would never have been known.

Breathlessly we listened whenever my brother would relate the story, which he did not at all enjoy doing, for a cutlass had been swung over his head, and his life threatened by the pirate's boatswain, demanding more money, after all had been taken. A Genoese messmate, Iachimo, shortened to plain "Jack" by the "Mexican's" crew, came to see my brother one day, and at the dinner table he went through the whole adventure in pantomime, which we children watched with wide-eyed terror and amusement. For there was some comedy mixed with what had been so nearly a tragedy, and Jack made us see the very whites of the black cook's eyes, who, favored by his color, had hidden himself — all except that dilated whiteness — between two great casks in the hold. Jack himself had fallen through a trap-door, was badly hurt, and could not extricate himself.

It was very ludicrous. Jack crept under the table to show us how he and the cook made eyes at each other down there in the darkness, not daring to speak. The pantomime was necessary, for the Genoese had very little English at his command.

When the pirate crew were brought into Salem for trial, my brother had the questionable satisfaction of identifying in the court-room the ruffian of a boatswain who had threatened his life. This boatswain and several others of the crew were executed in Boston. The boy found his brief sailor-experience quite enough for him, and afterward settled down quietly to the trade of a carpenter.

Changes thickened in the air around us. Not the least among them was the burning of " our meeting-house," in which we had all been baptized. One Sunday morning we children were told, when we woke, that we could not go to meeting that day, because the church was a heap of smoking ruins. It seemed to me almost like the end of the world.

During my father's life, a few years before my birth, his thoughts had been turned towards the new manufacturing town growing up on the banks of the Merrimack. He had once taken a journey there, with the possibility in his mind of making the place his home, his limited income furnishing no adequate promise of a maintenance for his large family of daughters. From the beginning, Lowell had a high reputation for good order, morality, piety, and all that was dear to the old-fashioned New Englander's heart.

After his death, my mother's thoughts naturally

followed the direction his had taken ; and seeing no other opening for herself, she sold her small estate, and moved to Lowell, with the intention of taking a corporation-house for mill-girl boarders. Some of the family objected, for the Old World traditions about factory life were anything but attractive ; and they were current in New England until the experiment at Lowell had shown that independent and intelligent workers invariably give their own character to their occupation. My mother had visited Lowell, and she was willing and glad, knowing all about the place, to make it our home.

The change involved a great deal of work. "Boarders" signified a large house, many beds, and an indefinite number of people. Such piles of sewing accumulated before us ! A sewing-bee, volunteered by the neighbors, reduced the quantity a little, and our child-fingers had to take their part. But the seams of those sheets did look to me as if they were miles long !

My sister Lida and I had our "stint," — so much to do every day. It was warm weather, and that made it the more tedious, for we wanted to be running about the fields we were so soon to leave. One day, in sheer desperation, we dragged a sheet up with us into an apple-tree in the yard, and sat and sewed there through the summer afternoon, beguiling the irksomeness of our task by telling stories and guessing riddles.

It was hardest for me to leave the garret and the garden. In the old houses the garret was the children's castle. The rough rafters, — it was always an unfinished room, otherwise not a true garret, — the music of the rain on the roof, the worn sea - chests with their miscellaneous treasures, the blue-roofed cradle that had sheltered ten blue-eyed babies, the tape-looms and reels and spinning-wheels, the herby smells, and the delightful dream corners, — these could not be taken with us to the new home. Wonderful people had looked out upon us from under those garret-eaves. Sindbad the Sailor and Baron Munchausen had sometimes strayed in and told us their unbelievable stories; and we had there made acquaintance with the great Caliph Haroun Alraschid.

To go away from the little garden was almost as bad. Its lilacs and peonies were beautiful to me, and in a corner of it was one tiny square of earth that I called my own, where I was at liberty to pull up my pinks and lady's delights every day, to see whether they had taken root, and where I could give my lazy morning-glory seeds a poke, morning after morning, to help them get up and begin their climb. Oh, I should miss the garden very much indeed!

It did not take long to turn over the new leaf of our home experience. One sunny day three of us children, my youngest sister, my brother John, and I, took with my mother the first stage-coach journey of our lives, across Lynnfield plains and over Andover hills to the banks of the Merrimack. We were set down before an empty house in a yet unfinished brick block, where we watched for the big wagon that was to bring our household goods.

It came at last; and the novelty of seeing our old furniture settled in new rooms kept us from being homesick. One after another they appeared, — bedsteads, chairs, tables, and, to me most welcome of all, the old mahogany secretary with brass-handled drawers, that had always stood in the " front room " at home. With it came the barrel full of books that had filled its shelves, and they took their places as naturally as if they had always lived in this strange town.

There they all stood again side by side on their shelves, the dear, dull, good old volumes that all my life I had tried in vain to take a sincere Sabbath-day interest in, — Scott's Commentaries on the Bible, Hervey's " Meditations," Young's "Night Thoughts," " Edwards on the Affections," and the Writings of Baxter and Doddridge. Besides these, there were bound volumes of the " Repository Tracts," which I had read and re-read; and the delightfully miscellaneous " Evangelicana," containing an account of Gilbert Tennent's wonderful trance; also the " History of the Spanish Inquisition," with some painfully realistic illustrations; a German Dictionary, whose outlandish letters and words I liked to puzzle myself over;

and a descriptive History of Hamburg, full of fine steel engravings — which last two or three volumes my father had brought with him from the countries to which he had sailed in his sea-faring days. A complete set of the " Missionary Herald," unbound, filled the upper shelves.

Other familiar articles journeyed with us : the brass-headed shovel and tongs, that it had been my especial task to keep bright; the two card-tables (which were as unacquainted as ourselves with ace, face, and trump) ; the two china mugs, with their eighteenth-century lady and gentleman figures, curiosities brought from over the sea; and reverently laid away by my mother with her choicest relics in the secretary-desk, my father's miniature, painted in Antwerp, a treasure only shown occasionally to us children as a holiday treat ; and my mother's easy-chair, — I should have felt as if I had lost *her*, had that been left behind. The earliest unexpressed ambition of my infancy had been to grow up and wear a cap, and sit in an easy-chair knitting, and look comfortable, just as my mother did.

Filled up with these things, the little 'one-windowed sitting-room easily caught the home feeling and gave it back to us. Inanimate objects do gather into themselves something of the character of those who live among them, through association ; and this alone makes heirlooms valuable. They are family treasures, because they are part of the family life, full of memories and inspirations. Bought or sold, they are nothing but old furniture. Nobody can buy the old associations; and nobody who has really felt how everything that has been in a home makes part of it, can willingly bargain away the old things.

My mother never thought of disposing of her best furniture, whatever her need. It traveled with her in every change of her abiding-place, as long as she lived, so that to us children home seemed to accompany her wherever she went. And, remaining yet in the family, it often brings back to me pleasant reminders of my childhood. No other Bible seems quite so sacred to me as the old Family Bible, out of which my father used to read when we were all gathered around him for worship. To turn its leaves and look at its pictures was one of our few Sabbath-day indulgences; and I cannot touch it now except with feelings of profound reverence.

For the first time in our lives, my little sister and I became pupils in a grammar school for both girls and boys, taught by a man. I was put with her into the sixth class, but was sent the very next day into the first. I did not belong in either, but somewhere between. And I was very uncomfortable in my promotion, for though the reading and spelling and grammar and geography were perfectly easy, I had never studied anything but mental arithmetic, and did not know

how to "do a sum." We had to show, when
called up to recite, a slateful of sums, "done" and
"proved." No explanations were ever asked of
us.

The girl who sat next to me saw my distress,
and offered to do my sums for me. I accepted
her proposal, feeling, however, that I was a miserable cheat. But I was afraid of the master,
who was tall and gaunt, and used to stalk across
the school-room, right over the desk-tops, to find
out if there was any mischief going on. Once,
having caught a boy annoying a seat-mate with a
pin, he punished the offender by pursuing him
around the school-room, sticking a pin into his
shoulder whenever he could overtake him. And
he had a fearful leather strap, which was sometimes used even upon the shrinking palm of a
little girl. If he should find out that I was a
pretender and deceiver, as I knew that I was, I
could not guess what might happen to me. He
never did, however. I was left unmolested in the
ignorance which I deserved. But I never liked
the girl who did my sums, and I fancied she had
a decided contempt for me.

There was a friendly looking boy always sitting
at the master's desk; they called him "the mon-
itor." It was his place to assist scholars who
were in trouble about their lessons, but I was too
bashful to speak to him, or to ask assistance of
anybody. I think that nobody learned much un-

der that régime, and the whole school system was soon after entirely reorganized.

Our house was quickly filled with a large feminine family. As a child, the gulf between little girlhood and young womanhood had always looked to me very wide. I supposed we should get across it by some sudden jump, by and by. But among these new companions of all ages, from fifteen to thirty years, we slipped into womanhood without knowing when or how.

Most of my mother's boarders were from New Hampshire and Vermont, and there was a fresh, breezy sociability about them which made them seem almost like a different race of beings from any we children had hitherto known.

We helped a little about the housework, before and after school, making beds, trimming lamps, and washing dishes. The heaviest work was done by a strong Irish girl, my mother always attending to the cooking herself. She was, however, a better caterer than the circumstances required or permitted. She liked to make nice things for the table, and, having been accustomed to an abundant supply, could never learn to economize. At a dollar and a quarter a week for board, (the price allowed for mill-girls by the corporations) great care in expenditure was necessary. It was not in my mother's nature closely to calculate costs, and in this way there came to be a continually increasing leak in the family purse.

The older members of the family did everything they could, but it was not enough. I heard it said one day, in a distressed tone, "The children will have to leave school and go into the mill."

There were many pros and cons between my mother and sisters before this was positively decided. The mill-agent did not want to take us two little girls, but consented on condition we should be sure to attend school the full number of months prescribed each year. I, the younger one, was then between eleven and twelve years old.

I listened to all that was said about it, very much fearing that I should not be permitted to do the coveted work. For the feeling had already frequently come to me, that I was the one too many in the overcrowded family nest. Once, before we left our old home, I had heard a neighbor condoling with my mother because there were so many of us, and her emphatic reply had been a great relief to my mind: —

"There is n't one more than I want. I could not spare a single one of my children."

But her difficulties were increasing, and I thought it would be a pleasure to feel that I was not a trouble or burden or expense to anybody. So I went to my first day's work in the mill with a light heart. The novelty of it made it seem easy, and it really was not hard, just to change the bobbins on the spinning-frames every **three** quarters of an hour or so, with half a dozen other little girls who were doing the same thing. When I came back at night, the family began to pity me for my long, tiresome day's work, but I laughed and said, —

"Why, it is nothing but fun. It is just like play."

And for a little while it was only a new amusement; I liked it better than going to school and "making believe" I was learning when I was not. And there was a great deal of play mixed with it. We were not occupied more than half the time. The intervals were spent frolicking around among the spinning-frames, teasing and talking to the older girls, or entertaining ourselves with games and stories in a corner, or exploring, with the overseer's permission, the mysteries of the carding-room, the dressing-room, and the weaving-room.

I never cared much for machinery. The buzzing and hissing and whizzing of pulleys and rollers and spindles and flyers around me often grew tiresome. I could not see into their complications, or feel interested in them. But in a room below us we were sometimes allowed to peer in through a sort of blind door at the great water-wheel that carried the works of the whole mill. It was so huge that we could only watch a few of its spokes at a time, and part of its dripping rim, moving with a slow, measured strength through the darkness that shut it in. It impressed me

with something of the awe which comes to us
in thinking of the great Power which keeps the
mechanism of the universe in motion.   Even
now, the remembrance of its large, mysterious
movement, in which every little motion of every
noisy little wheel was involved, brings back to me
a verse from one of my favorite hymns : —

> "Our lives through various scenes are drawn,
>   And vexed by trifling cares,
>   While Thine eternal thought moves on
>   Thy undisturbed affairs."

There were compensations for being shut in to
daily toil so early.   The mill itself had its lessons
for us.   But it was not, and could not be, the
right sort of life for a child, and we were happy
in the knowledge that, at the longest, our employment was only to be temporary.

When I took my next three months at the
grammar school, everything there was changed,
and I too was changed.   The teachers were kind,
and thorough in their instruction ; and my mind
seemed to have been ploughed up during that
year of work, so that knowledge took root in it
easily.   It was a great delight to me to study,
and at the end of the three months the master
told me that I was prepared for the high school.

But alas ! I could not go.   The little money I
could earn — one dollar a week, besides the price
of my board — was needed in the family, and I
must return to the mill.   It was a severe disap-

pointment to me, though I did not say so at home. I did not at all accept the conclusion of a neighbor whom I heard talking about it with my mother. His daughter was going to the high school, and my mother was telling him how sorry she was that I could not.

"Oh," he said, in a soothing tone, "my girl has n't got any such head - piece as yours has. Your girl does n't need to go."

Of course I knew that whatever sort of a "head-piece" I had, I did need and want just that very opportunity to study. I think the resolution was then formed, inwardly, that I *would* go to school again, some time, whatever happened. I went back to my work, but now without enthusiasm. I had looked through an open door that I was not willing to see shut upon me.

I began to reflect upon life rather seriously for a girl of twelve or thirteen. What was I here for? What could I make of myself? Must I submit to be carried along with the current, and do just what everybody else did? No: I knew I should not do that, for there was a certain Myself who was always starting up with her own original plan or aspiration before me, and who was quite indifferent as to what people generally thought.

Well, I would find out what this Myself was good for, and that she should be!

It was but the presumption of extreme youth.

How gladly would I know now, after these long years, just why I was sent into the world, and whether I have in any degree fulfilled the purpose of my being!

In the older times it was seldom said to little girls, as it always has been said to boys, that they ought to have some definite plan, while they were children, what to be and do when they were grown up. There was usually but one path open before them, to become good wives and housekeepers. And the ambition of most girls was to follow their mothers' footsteps in this direction; a natural and laudable ambition. But girls, as well as boys, must often have been conscious of their own peculiar capabilities, — must have desired to cultivate and make use of their individual powers. When I was growing up, they had already begun to be encouraged to do so. We were often told that it was our duty to develop any talent we might possess, or at least to learn how to do some one thing which the world needed, or which would make it a pleasanter world.

When I thought what I should best like to do, my first dream — almost a baby's dream — about it was that it would be a fine thing to be a schoolteacher, like Aunt Hannah. Afterward, when I heard that there were artists, I wished I could some time be one. A slate and pencil, to draw pictures, was my first request whenever a day's ailment kept me at home from school; and I rather enjoyed being a little ill, for the sake of amusing myself in that way. The wish grew up with me; but there were no good drawing-teachers in those days, and if there had been, the cost of instruction would have been beyond the family means. My sister Emilie, however, who saw my taste and shared it herself, did her best to assist me, furnishing me with pencil and paper and paint-box.

If I could only make a rose bloom on paper, I thought I should be happy! or if I could at last succeed in drawing the outline of winter-stripped boughs as I saw them against the sky, it seemed to me that I should be willing to spend years in trying. I did try a little, and very often. Jack Frost was my most inspiring teacher. His sketches on the bedroom window-pane in cold mornings were my ideal studies of Swiss scenery, crags and peaks and chalets and fir-trees, — and graceful tracery of ferns, like those that grew in the woods where we went huckleberrying, all blended together by his touch of enchantment. I wondered whether human fingers ever succeeded in imitating that lovely work.

The taste has followed me all my life through, but I could never indulge it except as a recreation. I was not to be an artist, and I am rather glad that I was hindered, for I had even stronger inclinations in other directions; and art, really noble art, requires the entire devotion of a lifetime.

I seldom thought seriously of becoming an author, although it seemed to me that anybody who had written a book would have a right to feel very proud. But I believed that a person must be exceedingly wise, before presuming to attempt it : although now and then I thought I could feel ideas growing in my mind that it might be worth while to put into a book, — if I lived and studied until I was forty or fifty years old.

I wrote my little verses, to be sure, but that was nothing; they just grew. They were the same as breathing or singing. I could not help writing them, and I thought and dreamed a great many that never were put on paper. They seemed to fly into my mind and away again, like birds going with a carol through the air. It seemed strange to me that people should notice them, or should think my writing verses anything peculiar ; for I supposed that they were in everybody's mind, just as they were in mine, and that anybody could write them who chose.

One day I heard a relative say to my mother, —

" Keep what she writes till she grows up, and perhaps she will get money for it. I have heard of somebody who earned a thousand dollars by writing poetry."

It sounded so absurd to me. Money for writing verses ! One dollar would be as ridiculous as a thousand. I should as soon have thought of being paid for thinking! My mother, fortunately, was sensible enough never to flatter me or let me be flattered about my scribbling. It never was allowed to hinder any work I had to do. I crept away into a corner to write what came into my head, just as I ran away to play; and I looked upon it only as my most agreeable amusement, never thinking of preserving anything which did not of itself stay in my memory. This too was well, for the time did not come when I could afford to look upon verse-writing as an occupation. Through my life, it has only been permitted to me as an aside from other more pressing employments. Whether I should have written better verses had circumstances left me free to do what I chose, it is impossible now to know.

All my thoughts about my future sent me back to Aunt Hannah and my first infantile idea of being a teacher. I foresaw that I should be that before I could be or do anything else. It had been impressed upon me that I must make myself useful in the world, and certainly one could be useful who could "keep school" as Aunt Hannah did. I did not see anything else for a girl to do who wanted to use her brains as well as her hands. So the plan of preparing myself to be a teacher gradually and almost unconsciously shaped itself in my mind as the only practicable one. I could earn my living in that way, — an all-important consideration.

I liked the thought of self-support, but I would have chosen some artistic or beautiful work if I could. I had no especial aptitude for teaching, and no absorbing wish to be a teacher, but it seemed to me that I might succeed if I tried. What I did like about it was that one must know something first. I must acquire knowledge before I could impart it, and that was just what I wanted. I could be a student, wherever I was and whatever else I had to be or do, and I would!

I knew I should write; I could not help doing that, for my hand seemed instinctively to move towards pen and paper in moments of leisure. But to write anything worth while, I must have mental cultivation; so, in preparing myself to teach, I could also be preparing myself to write.

This was the plan that indefinitely shaped itself in my mind as I returned to my work in the spinning-room, and which I followed out, not without many breaks and hindrances and neglects, during the next six or seven years, — to learn all I could, so that I should be fit to teach or to write, as the way opened. And it turned out that fifteen or twenty of my best years were given to teaching.

VIII.

IT did not take us younger ones long to get acquainted with our new home, and to love it.

To live beside a river had been to me a child's dream of romance. Rivers, as I pictured them, came down from the mountains, and were born in the clouds. They were bordered by green meadows, and graceful trees leaned over to gaze into their bright mirrors. Our shallow tidal creek was the only river I had known, except as visioned on the pages of the " Pilgrim's Progress," and in the Book of Revelation. And the Merrimack was like a continuation of that dream.

I soon made myself familiar with the rocky nooks along Pawtucket Falls, shaded with hemlocks and white birches. Strange new wild flowers grew beside the rushing waters, — among them Sir Walter Scott's own harebells, which I had never thought of except as blossoms of poetry ; here they were, as real to me as to his Lady of the Lake ! I loved the harebell, the first new flower the river gave me, as I had never loved a flower before.

There was but one summer holiday for us who

worked in the mills — the Fourth of July. We made a point of spending it out of doors, making excursions down the river to watch the meeting of the slow Concord and the swift Merrimack; or around by the old canal-path, to explore the mysteries of the Guard Locks; or across the bridge, clambering up Dracut Heights, to look away to the dim blue mountains.

On that morning it was our custom to wake one another at four o'clock, and start off on a tramp together over some retired road whose chief charm was its unfamiliarity, returning to a very late breakfast, with draggled gowns and aprons full of dewy wild roses. No matter if we must get up at five the next morning and go back to our humdrum toil, we should have the roses to take with us for company, and the sweet air of the woodland which lingered about them would scent our thoughts all day, and make us forget the oily smell of the machinery.

We were children still, whether at school or at work, and Nature still held us close to her motherly heart. Nature came very close to the mill-gates, too, in those days. There was green grass all around them; violets and wild geraniums grew by the canals; and long stretches of open land between the corporation buildings and the street made the town seem country-like.

The slope behind our mills (the "Lawrence" Mills) was a green lawn; and in front of some of them the overseers had gay flower-gardens; we passed in to our work through a splendor of dahlias and hollyhocks.

The gray stone walls of St. Anne's church and rectory made a picturesque spot in the middle of the town, remaining still as a lasting monument to the religious purpose which animated the first manufacturers. The church arose close to the oldest corporation (the " Merrimack "), and seemed a part of it, and a part, also, of the original idea of the place itself, which was always a city of worshipers, although it came to be filled with a population which preferred meeting-houses to churches. I admired the church greatly. I had never before seen a real one; never anything but a plain frame meeting-house; and it and its benign, apostolic-looking rector were like a leaf out of an English story-book.

And so, also, was the tiny white cottage nearly opposite, set in the middle of a pretty flower-garden that sloped down to the canal. In the garden there was almost always a sweet little girl in a pink gown and white sunbonnet gathering flowers when I passed that way, and I often went out of my path to do so. These relieved the monotony of the shanty-like shops which bordered the main street. The town had sprung up with a mushroom-rapidity, and there was no attempt at veiling the newness of its bricks and mortar, its boards and paint.

But there were buildings that had their own individuality, and asserted it. One of these was a mud-cabin with a thatched roof, that looked as if it had emigrated bodily from the bogs of Ireland. It had settled itself down into a green hollow by the roadside, and it looked as much at home with the lilac-tinted crane's-bill and yellow buttercups as if it had never lost sight of the shamrocks of Erin.

Now, too, my childish desire to see a real beggar was gratified. Straggling petitioners for " cold victuals " hung around our back yard, always of Hibernian extraction; and a slice of bread was rewarded with a shower of benedictions that lost itself upon us in the flood of its own incomprehensible brogue.

Some time every summer a fleet of canoes would glide noiselessly up the river, and a company of Penobscot Indians would land at a green point almost in sight from our windows. Pawtucket Falls had always been one of their favorite camping-places. Their strange endeavors to combine civilization with savagery were a great source of amusement to us; men and women clad alike in loose gowns, stove-pipe hats, and moccasons ; grotesque relics of aboriginal forest-life. The sight of these uncouth-looking red men made the romance fade entirely out of the Indian stories we had heard. Still their wigwam camp was a show we would not willingly have missed.

The transition from childhood to girlhood, when a little girl has had an almost unlimited freedom of out-of-door life, is practically the toning down of a mild sort of barbarianism, and is often attended by a painfully awkward self-consciousness. I had an innate dislike of conventionalities. I clung to the child's inalienable privilege of running half wild; and when I found that I really was growing up, I felt quite rebellious.

I was as tall as a woman at thirteen, and my older sisters insisted upon lengthening my dresses, and putting up my mop of hair with a comb. I felt injured and almost outraged because my protestations against this treatment were unheeded; and when the transformation in my visible appearance was effected, I went away by myself and had a good cry, which I would not for the world have had them know about, as that would have added humiliation to my distress. And the greatest pity about it was that I too soon became accustomed to the situation. I felt like a child, but considered it my duty to think and behave like a woman. I began to look upon it as a very serious thing to live. The untried burden seemed already to have touched my shoulders. For a time I was morbidly self-critical, and at the same time extremely reserved. The associates I chose were usually grave young women, ten or fifteen years older than myself; but I think I felt older and appeared older than they did.

Childhood, however, is not easily defrauded of its birthright, and mine soon reasserted itself. At home I was among children of my own age, for some cousins and other acquaintances had come to live and work with us. We had our evening frolics and entertainments together, and we always made the most of our brief holiday hours. We had also with us now the sister Emilie of my fairy-tale memories, who had grown into a strong, earnest-hearted woman. We all looked up to her as our model, and the ideal of our heroine-worship; for our deference to her in every way did amount to that.

She watched over us, gave us needed reproof and commendation, rarely cosseted us, but rather made us laugh at what many would have considered the hardships of our lot. She taught us not only to accept the circumstances in which we found ourselves, but to win from them courage and strength. When we came in shivering from our work, through a snow-storm, complaining of numb hands and feet, she would say cheerily, "But it does n't make you any warmer to *say* you are cold;" and this was typical of the way she took life generally, and tried to have us take it. She was constantly denying herself for our sakes, without making us feel that she was doing so. But she did not let us get into the bad habit of pitying ourselves because we were not as "well off" as many other children. And indeed we considered ourselves pleasantly situated; but the best of it all was that we had *her*.

Her theories for herself, and her practice, too, were rather severe; but we tried to follow them, according to our weaker abilities. Her custom was, for instance, to take a full cold bath every morning before she went to her work, even though the water was chiefly broken ice; and we did the same whenever we could be resolute enough. It required both nerve and will to do this at five o'olock on a zero morning, in a room without a fire; but it helped us to harden ourselves, while we formed a good habit. The working-day in winter began at the very earliest daylight, and ended at half-past seven in the evening.

Another habit of hers was to keep always beside her at her daily work something to study or to think about. At first it was "Watts on the Improvement of the Mind," arranged as a text-book, with questions and answers, by the minister of Beverly who had made the thought of the millennium such a reality to his people. She quite wore this book out, carrying it about with her in her working-dress pocket. After that, "Locke on the Understanding" was used in the same way. She must have known both books through and through by heart. Then she read Combe and Abercrombie, and discussed their physics and metaphysics with our girl boarders, some of whom had remarkably acute and well-balanced minds. Her own seemed to have turned from its early bent toward the romantic, her taste being now for serious and practical, though sometimes abstruse, themes. I remember that Young and Pollok were her favorite poets.

I could not keep up with her in her studies and readings, for many of the books she liked seemed to me very dry. I did not easily take to the argumentative or moralizing method, which I came to regard as a proof of the weakness of my own intellect in comparison with hers. I would gladly have kept pace with her if I could. Anything under the heading of " Didactick," like some of the pieces in the old " English Reader," used by school-children in the generation just before ours, always repelled me. But I thought it necessary to discipline myself by reading such pieces, and my first attempt at prose composition, " On Friendship," was stiffly modeled after a certain " Didactick Essay " in that same English Reader.

My sister, however, cared more to watch the natural development of our minds than to make us follow the direction of hers. She was really our teacher, although she never assumed that position. Certainly I learned more from her about my own capabilities, and how I might put them to use, than I could have done at any school we knew of, had it been possible for me to attend one.

I think she was determined that we should not

be mentally defrauded by the circumstances which had made it necessary for us to begin so early to win our daily bread. This remark applies especially to me, as my older sisters (only two or three of them had come to Lowell) soon drifted away from us into their own new homes or occupations, and she and I were left together amid the whir of spindles and wheels.

One thing she planned for us, her younger housemates, — a dozen or so of cousins, friends, and sisters, some attending school, and some at work in the mill, — was a little fortnightly paper, to be filled with our original contributions, she herself acting as editor.

I do not know where she got the idea, unless it was from Mrs. Lydia Maria Child's "Juvenile Miscellany," which had found its way to us some years before, — a most delightful guest, and, I think, the first magazine prepared for American children, who have had so many since then. (I have always been glad that I knew that sweet woman with the child's heart and the poet's soul, in her later years, and could tell her how happy she had helped to make my childhood.) Our little sheet was called "The Diving Bell," probably from the sea-associations of the name. We kept our secrets of authorship very close from everybody except the editor, who had to decipher the handwriting and copy the pieces. It was, indeed, an important part of the fun to guess who wrote particular pieces. After a little while, however, our mannerisms betrayed us. One of my cousins was known to be the chief story-teller, and I was recognized as the leading rhymer among the younger contributors; the editor-sister excelling in her versifying, as she did in almost everything.

It was a cluster of very conscious-looking little girls that assembled one evening in the attic room, chosen on account of its remoteness from intruders (for we did not admit even the family as a public; the writers themselves were the only audience); to listen to the reading of our first paper. We took Saturday evening, because that was longer than the other work-day evenings, the mills being closed earlier. Such guessing and wondering and admiring as we had! But nobody would acknowledge her own work, for that would have spoiled the pleasure. Only there were certain wise hints and maxims that we knew never came from any juvenile head among us, and those we set down as " editorials."

Some of the stories contained rather remarkable incidents. One, written to illustrate a little girl's habit of carelessness about her own special belongings, told of her rising one morning, and after hunting around for her shoes half an hour or so, finding them *in the book-case*, where she had *accidentally locked them up* the night before!

To convince myself that I could write something besides rhymes, I had attempted an essay of half a column on a very extensive subject, " MIND." It began loftily :—
" What a noble and beautiful thing is mind ! " and it went on in the same high-flown strain to no particular end. But the editor praised it, after having declined the verdict of the audience that she was its author ; and I felt sufficiently flattered by both judgments.

I wrote more rhymes than anything else, because they came more easily. But I always felt that the ability to write good prose was far more desirable, and it seems so to me still. I will give my little girl readers a single specimen of my twelve-year-old " Diving Bell " verses, though I feel as if I ought to apologize even for that. It is on a common subject, " Life like a Rose " : —

> Childhood 's like a tender bud
>   That 's scarce been formed an hour,
> But which erelong will doubtless be
>   A bright and lovely flower.
>
> And youth is like a full-blown rose
>   Which has not known decay ;
> But which must soon, alas ! too soon !
>   Wither and fade away.
>
> And age is like a withered rose,
>   That bends beneath the blast ;
> But though its beauty all is gone,
>   Its fragrance yet may last.

This, and other verses that I wrote then, serve
to illustrate the child's usual inclination to look
forward meditatively, rather than to think and
write of the simple things that belong to children.

Our small venture set some of us imagining
what larger possibilities might be before us in
the far future. We talked over the things we
should like to do when we should be women out
in the active world; and the author of the shoe-
story horrified us by declaring that she meant to
be distinguished when she grew up for something, even if it was for something bad! She did
go so far in a bad way as to plagiarize a long
poem in a subsequent number of the " Diving
Bell "; but the editor found her out, and we all
thought that a reproof from Emilie was suffi-
cient punishment.

I do not know whether it was fortunate or un-
fortunate for me that I had not, by nature, what
is called literary ambition. I knew that I had a
knack at rhyming, and I knew that I enjoyed
nothing better than to try to put thoughts and
words together, in any way. But I did it for the
pleasure of rhyming and writing, indifferent as
to what might come of it. For any one who could
take hold of every-day, practical work, and carry
it on successfully, I had a profound respect. To
be what is called "capable" seemed to me better
worth while than merely to have a taste or talent

for writing, perhaps because I was conscious of my deficiencies in the former respect. But certainly the world needs deeds more than it needs words. I should never have been willing to be *only* a writer, without using my hands to some good purpose besides.

My sister, however, told me that here was a talent which I had no right to neglect, and which I ought to make the most of. I believed in her; I thought she understood me better than I understood myself; and it was a comfort to be assured that my scribbling was not wholly a waste of time. So I used pencil and paper in every spare minute I could find.

Our little home-journal went bravely on through twelve numbers. Its yellow manuscript pages occasionally meet my eyes when I am rummaging among my ōld papers, with the half-conscious look of a waif that knows it has no right to its escape from the waters of oblivion.

While it was in progress my sister Emilie became acquainted with a family of bright girls, near neighbors of ours, who proposed that we should join with them, and form a little society for writing and discussion, to meet fortnightly at their house. We met, — I think I was the youngest of the group, — prepared a Constitution and By-Laws, and named ourselves "The Improvement Circle." If I remember rightly, my sister was our first president. The older ones talked and wrote on many subjects quite above me. I was shrinkingly bashful, as half-grown girls usually are, but I wrote my little essays and read them, and listened to the rest, and enjoyed it all exceedingly. Out of this little " Improvement Circle " grew the larger one whence issued the " Lowell Offering," a year or two later.

At this time I had learned to do a spinner's work, and I obtained permission to tend some frames that stood directly in front of the river-windows, with only them and the wall behind me, extending half the length of the mill, — and one young woman beside me, at the farther end of the row. She was a sober, mature person, who scarcely thought it worth her while to speak often to a child like me; and I was, when with strangers, rather a reserved girl; so I kept myself occupied with the river, my work, and my thoughts. And the river and my thoughts flowed on together, the happiest of companions. Like a loitering pilgrim, it sparkled up to me in recognition as it glided along, and bore away my little frets and fatigues on its bosom. When the work " went well," I sat in the window-seat, and let my fancies fly whither they would, — downward to the sea, or upward to the hills that hid the mountain-cradle of the Merrimack.

The printed regulations forbade us to bring books into the mill, so I made my window-seat into a small library of poetry, pasting its side all over with newspaper clippings. In those days we had only weekly papers, and they had always a " poet's corner," where standard writers were well represented, with anonymous ones, also. I was not, of course, much of a critic. I chose my verses for their sentiment, and because I wanted to commit them to memory; sometimes it was a long poem, sometimes a hymn, sometimes only a stray verse. Mrs. Hemans sang with me, —

" Far away, o'er the blue hills far away ; "

and I learned and loved her " Better Land," and

" If thou hast crushed a flower,"

and " Kindred Hearts."

I wonder if Miss Landon really did write that fine poem to Mont Blanc which was printed in her volume, but which sounds so entirely unlike everything else she wrote! This was one of my window-gems. It ended with the appeal, —

" Alas for thy past mystery !
For thine untrodden snow !
Nurse of the tempest ! hast thou none
To guard thine outraged brow ? "

and it contained a stanza that I often now repeat to myself : —

" We know too much : scroll after scroll
Weighs down our weary shelves :
Our only point of ignorance
Is centred in ourselves."

There was one anonymous waif in my collection that I was very fond of. I have never seen it since, nor ever had the least clue to its authorship. It stirred me and haunted me; and it often comes back to me now, in snatches like these: —

> "The human mind! That lofty thing,
>   The palace and the throne
> Where Reason sits, a sceptred king,
>   And breathes his judgment-tone!

> "The human soul! That startling thing,
>   Mysterious and sublime;
> An angel sleeping on the wing,
>   Worn by the scoffs of time.
> From heaven in tears to earth it stole —
> That startling thing, the human soul."

I was just beginning, in my questionings as to the meaning of life, to get glimpses of its true definition from the poets, — that it is love, service, the sacrifice of self for others' good. The lesson was slowly learned, but every hint of it went to my heart, and I kept in sight upon my window wall reminders like that of holy George Herbert: —

> "Be useful where thou livest, that they may
> Both want and wish thy pleasing presence still.
>   — Find out men's wants and will,
> And meet them there. All worldly joys go less
> To the one joy of doing kindnesses;"

and that well-known passage from Talfourd, —

> "The blessings which the weak and poor can scatter,
> Have their own season.
> It is a little thing to speak a phrase
> Of common comfort, which, by daily use,
> Has almost lost its sense; yet on the ear
> Of him who thought to die unmourned 't will fall
> Like choicest music."

A very familiar extract from Carlos Wilcox, almost the only quotation made nowadays from his poems, was often on my sister Emilie's lips, whose heart seemed always to be saying to itself : —

"Pour blessings round thee like a shower of gold ! "

I had that beside me, too, and I copy part of it here, for her sake, and because it will be good for my girl readers to keep in mind one of the noblest utterances of an almost forgotten American poet : —

"Rouse to some work of high and holy love,
     And thou an angel's happiness shalt know ;
Shalt bless the earth while in the world above.
The good begun by thee shall onward flow.
The pure, sweet stream shall deeper, wider grow.
The seed that in these few and fleeting hours
     Thy hands, unsparing and unwearied sow,
Shall deck thy grave with amaranthine flowers,
And yield thee fruits divine in heaven's immortal bowers."

One great advantage which came to these many stranger girls through being brought together, away from their own homes, was that it taught them to go out of themselves, and enter into the lives of others.   Home-life, when one always stays at home, is necessarily narrowing.   That is one reason why so many women are petty and unthoughtful of any except their own family's interests.   We have hardly begun to live until we can take in the idea of the whole human family as the one to which we truly belong.   To me, it was an incalculable help to find myself among so many

working-girls, all of us thrown upon our own resources, but thrown much more upon each others'
sympathies.

And the stream beside which we toiled added
to its own inspirations human suggestions drawn
from our acquaintance with each other. It
blended itself with the flow of our lives. Almost
the first of my poemlets in the "Lowell Offering" was entitled "The River." These are some
lines of it : —

> Gently flowed a river bright
> On its path of liquid light,
> Gleaming now soft banks between,
> Winding now through valleys green,
> Cheering with its presence mild
> Cultured fields and woodlands wild.
>
> Is not such a pure one's life ?
> Ever shunning pride and strife,
> Noiselessly along she goes,
> Known by gentle deeds she does ;
> Often wandering far, to bless,
> And do others kindnesses.
>
> Thus, by her own virtues shaded,
> While pure thoughts, like starbeams, lie
> Mirrored in her heart and eye,
> She, content to be unknown,
> All serenely moveth on,
> Till, released from Time's commotion,
> Self is lost in Love's wide ocean.

There was many a young girl near me whose
life was like the beautiful course of the river in
my ideal of her. The Merrimack has blent its

music with the onward song of many a lovely soul that, clad in plain working-clothes, moved heavenward beside its waters.

One of the loveliest persons I ever knew was a young girl who worked opposite to me in the spinning-room. Our eyes made us friends long before we spoke to each other. She was an orphan, well-bred and well-educated, about twenty years old, and she had brought with her to her place of toil the orphan child of her sister, left to her as a death-bed legacy. They boarded with a relative. The factory boarding-houses were often managed by families of genuine refinement, as in this case, and the one comfort of Caroline's life was her beautiful little niece, to whom she could go home when the day's work was over.

Her bereavements had given an appealing sadness to her whole expression; but she had accepted them and her changed circumstances with the submission of profound faith which everybody about her felt in everything she said and did. I think I first knew, through her, how character can teach, without words. To see her and her little niece together was almost like looking at a picture of the Madonna. Caroline afterwards became an inmate of my mother's family, and we were warm friends until her death a few years ago.

Some of the girls could not believe that the Bible was meant to be counted among forbidden books. We all thought that the Scriptures had a right to go wherever we went, and that if we needed them anywhere, it was at our work. I evaded the law by carrying some leaves from a torn Testament in my pocket.

The overseer, caring more for law than gospel, confiscated all he found. He had his desk full of Bibles. It sounded oddly to hear him say to the most religious girl in the room, when he took hers away, " I did think you had more conscience than to bring that book here." But we had some close ethical questions to settle in those days. It was a rigid code of morality under which we lived. Nobody complained of it, however, and we were doubtless better off for its strictness, in the end.

The last window in the row behind me was filled with flourishing house-plants — fragrant-leaved geraniums, the overseer's pets. They gave that corner a bowery look; the perfume and freshness tempted me there often. Standing before that window, I could look across the room and see girls moving backwards and forwards among the spinning-frames, sometimes stooping, sometimes reaching up their arms, as their work required, with easy and not ungraceful movements. On the whole, it was far from being a disagreeable place to stay in. The girls were bright-looking and neat, and everything was kept clean and shining. The effect of the whole was rather attractive to strangers.

My grandfather came to see my mother once at about this time and visited the mills. When he had entered our room, and looked around for a moment, he took off his hat and made a low bow to the girls, first toward the right, and then toward the left. We were familiar with his courteous habits, partly due to his French descent; but we had never seen anybody bow to a room full of mill girls in that polite way, and some one of the family afterwards asked him why he did so. He looked a little surprised at the question, but answered promptly and with dignity, "I always take off my hat to ladies."

His courtesy was genuine. Still, we did not call ourselves ladies. We did not forget that we were working-girls, wearing coarse aprons suitable to our work, and that there was some danger of our becoming drudges. I know that sometimes the confinement of the mill became very wearisome to me. In the sweet June weather I would lean far out of the window, and try not to hear the unceasing clash of sound inside. Looking away to the hills, my whole stifled being would cry out

"Oh, that I had wings!"

Still I was there from choice, and

" The prison unto which we doom ourselves,
No prison is."

And I was every day making discoveries about life, and about myself. I had naturally some

elements of the recluse, and would never, of my
own choice, have lived in a crowd. I loved quietness. The noise of machinery was particularly dis-
tasteful to me. But I found that the crowd was
made up of single human lives, not one of them
wholly uninteresting, when separately known. I
learned also that there are many things which
belong to the whole world of us together, that
no one of us, nor any few of us, can claim or
enjoy for ourselves alone. I discovered, too, that
I could so accustom myself to the noise that it
became like a silence to me. And I defied the
machinery to make me its slave. Its incessant dis-
cords could not drown the music of my thoughts
if I would let them fly high enough. Even the
long hours, the early rising, and the regularity
enforced by the clangor of the bell were good
discipline for one who was naturally inclined to
dally and to dream, and who loved her own personal liberty with a willful rebellion against control. Perhaps I could have brought myself into
the limitations of order and method in no other
way.

Like a plant that starts up in showers and sunshine and does not know which has best helped
it to grow, it is difficult to say whether the hard
things or the pleasant things did me most good.
But when I was sincerest with myself, as also
when I thought least about it, I know that I was
glad to be alive, and to be just where I was.

It is a conquest when we can lift ourselves above the annoyances of circumstances over which we have no control ; but it is a greater victory when we can make those circumstances our helpers, — when we can appreciate the good there is in them. It has often seemed to me as if Life stood beside me, looking me in the face, and saying, " Child, you must learn to like me in the form in which you see me, before I can offer myself to you in any other aspect."

It was so with this disagreeable necessity of living among many people. There is nothing more miserable than to lose the feeling of our own distinctiveness, since that is our only clue to the Purpose behind us and the End before us. But when we have discovered that human beings are not a mere " mass," but an orderly Whole, of which we are a part, it is all so different !

This we working-girls might have learned from the webs of cloth we saw woven around us. Every little thread must take its place as warp or woof, and keep in it steadily. Left to itself, it would be only a loose, useless filament. Trying to wander in an independent or a disconnected way among the other threads, it would make of the whole web an inextricable snarl. Yet each little thread must be as firmly spun as if it were the only one, or the result would be a worthless fabric.

That we are entirely separate, while yet we entirely belong to the Whole, is a truth that we learn to rejoice in, as we come to understand more and more of ourselves, and of this human life of ours, which seems so complicated, and yet is so simple. And when we once get a glimpse of the Divine Plan in it all, and know that to be just where we are, doing just what we are doing just at this hour because it is our appointed hour, — when we become aware that this is the very best thing possible for us in God's universe, the hard task grows easy, the tiresome employment welcome and delightful. Having fitted ourselves to our present work in such a way as this, we are usually prepared for better work, and are sent to take a better place.

Perhaps this is one of the unfailing laws of progress in our being. Perhaps the Master of Life always rewards those who do their little faithfully by giving them some greater opportunity for faithfulness. Certainly, it is a comfort, wherever we are, to say to ourselves: —

> "Thou camest not to thy place by accident,
> It is the very place God meant for thee."

IX.

THE pleasure we found in making new acquaintances among our workmates arose partly from their having come from great distances, regions unknown to us, as the northern districts of Maine and New Hampshire and Vermont were, in those days of stage-coach traveling, when railroads had as yet only connected the larger cities with one another.

It seemed wonderful to me to be talking with anybody who had really seen mountains and lived among them. One of the younger girls, who worked beside me during my very first days in the mill, had come from far up near the sources of the Merrimack, and she told me a great deal about her home, and about farm-life among the hills. I listened almost with awe when she said that she lived in a valley where the sun set at four o'clock, and where the great snow-storms drifted in so that sometimes they did not see a neighbor for weeks.

To have mountain-summits looking down upon one out of the clouds, summer and winter, by day and by night, seemed to me something both delightful and terrible. And yet here was this girl to whom it all appeared like the merest commonplace. What she felt about it was that it was " awful cold, sometimes; the days were so short! and it grew dark so early!" Then she told me about the spinning, and the husking, and the sugar-making, while we sat in a corner together, waiting to replace the full spools by empty ones, — the work usually given to the little girls.

I had a great admiration for this girl, because she had come from those wilderness-regions. The scent of pine - woods and checkerberry - leaves seemed to hang about her. I believe I liked her all the better because she said " daown " and " haow." It was part of the mountain-flavor.

I tried, on my part, to impress her with stories of the sea ; but I did not succeed very well. Her principal comment was, " They don't think much of sailors up *aour* way." And I received the impression, from her and others, and from my own imagination, that rural life was far more delightful than the life of towns.

But there is something in the place where we were born that holds us always by the heartstrings. A town that still has a great deal of the country in it, one that is rich in beautiful scenery and ancestral associations, is almost like a living being, with a body and a soul. We speak of such a town, if our birthplace, as of a mother, and think of ourselves as her sons and daughters.

So we felt, my sisters and I, about our dear native town of Beverly. Its miles of sea-border, almost every sunny cove and rocky headland of which was a part of some near relative's homestead, were only half a day's journey distant; and the misty ocean-spaces beyond still widened out on our imagination from the green inland landscape around us. But the hills sometimes shut us in, body and soul. To those who have been reared by the sea a wide horizon is a necessity, both for the mind and for the eye.

We had many opportunities of escape towards our native shores, for the larger part of our large family still remained there, and there was a constant coming and going among us. The stage-driver looked upon us as his especial charge, and we had a sense of personal property in the Salem and Lowell stage-coach, which had once, like a fairy-godmother's coach, rumbled down into our own little lane, taken possession of us, and carried us off to a new home.

My married sisters had families growing up about them, and they liked to have us younger ones come and help take care of their babies. One of them sent for me just when the close air and long days' work were beginning to tell upon my health, and it was decided that I had better go. The salt wind soon restored my strength, and those months of quiet family life were very good for me.

Like most young girls, I had a motherly fondness for little children, and my two baby-nephews were my pride and delight. The older one had a delicate constitution, and there was a thoughtful, questioning look in his eyes, that seemed to gaze forward almost sadly, and foresee that he should never attain to manhood. The younger, a plump, vigorous urchin, three or four months old, did, without doubt, "feel his life in every limb." He was my especial charge, for his brother's clinging weakness gave him, the first-born, the place nearest his mother's heart. The baby bore the family name, mine and his mother's; "our little Lark," we sometimes called him, for his wide-awakeness and his merry-heartedness. (Alas! neither of those beautiful boys grew up to be men! One page of my home-memories is sadly written over with their elegy, the "Graves of a Household." Father, mother, and four sons, an entire family, long since passed away from earthly sight.)

The tie between my lovely baby-nephew and myself became very close. The first two years of a child's life are its most appealing years, and call out all the latent tenderness of the nature on which it leans for protection. I think I should have missed one of the best educating influences of my youth, if I had not had the care of that baby for a year or more, just as I entered my

teens.   I was never so happy as when I held him
in my arms, sleeping or waking ; and he, happy
anywhere, was always contented when he was
with me.

I was as fond as ever of reading, and somehow
I managed to combine baby and book. Dickens's
" Old Curiosity Shop " was just then coming out
in a Philadelphia weekly paper, and I read it
with the baby playing at my feet, or lying across
my lap, in an unfinished room given up to sea-
chests and coffee-bags and spicy foreign odors.
(My cherub's papa was a sea - captain, usually
away on his African voyages.)   Little Nell and
her grandfather became as real to me as my
darling charge, and if a tear from his nurse's eyes
sometimes dropped upon his cheek as he slept, he
was not saddened by it.   When he awoke he was
irrepressible ; clutching at my hair with his stout
pink fists, and driving all dream-people effectually
out of my head.   Like all babies, he was something of a tyrant ; but that brief, sweet despotism
ends only too soon.   I put him gratefully down,
dimpled, chubby, and imperious, upon the list of
my girlhood's teachers.

My sister had no domestic help besides mine,
so I learned a good deal about general housework.   A girl's preparation for life was, in those
days, considered quite imperfect, who had no practical knowledge of that kind.   We were taught,
indeed, how to do everything that a woman might

be called upon to do under any circumstances, for herself or for the household she lived in. It was one of the advantages of the old simple way of living, that the young daughters of the house were, as a matter of course, instructed in all these things. They acquired the habit of being ready for emergencies, and the family that required no outside assistance was delightfully independent.

A young woman would have been considered a very inefficient being who could not make and mend and wash and iron her own clothing, and get three regular meals and clear them away every day, besides keeping the house tidy, and doing any other needed neighborly service, such as sitting all night by a sick-bed. To be "a good watcher" was considered one of the most important of womanly attainments. People who lived side by side exchanged such services without waiting to be asked, and they seemed to be, happiest of whom such kindnesses were most expected.

Every kind of work brings its own compensations and attractions. I really began to like plain sewing; I enjoyed sitting down for a whole afternoon of it, fingers flying and thoughts flying faster still, — the motion of the hands seeming to set the mind astir. Such afternoons used to bring me throngs of poetic suggestions, particularly if I sat by an open window and could hear the wind blowing and a bird or two singing. Nature is often very generous in opening her heart to those

who must keep their hands employed.   Perhaps
it is because she is always quietly at work herself,
and so sympathizes with her busy human friends.
And possibly there is no needful occupation
which is wholly unbeautiful.   The beauty of work
depends upon the way we meet it — whether we
arm ourselves each morning to attack it as an en-
emy that must be vanquished before night comes,
or whether we open our eyes with the sunrise to
welcome it as an approaching friend who will keep
us delightful company all day, and who will make
us feel, at evening, that the day was well worth
its fatigues.

I found my practical experience of housekeeping and baby-tending very useful to me afterwards at the West, in my sister Emilie's family,
when she was disabled by illness.   I think, indeed,
that every item of real knowledge I ever acquired
has come into use somewhere or somehow in the
course of the years.   But these were not the things
I had most wished to do.   The whole world of
thought lay unexplored before me, — a world of
which I had already caught large and tempting
glimpses, and I did not like to feel the horizon
shutting me in, even to so pleasant a corner as
this.   And the worst of it was that I was getting too easy and contented, too indifferent to the
higher realities which my work and my thoughtful
companions had kept keenly clear before me.   I
felt myself slipping into an inward apathy from

which it was hard to rouse myself. I could not let it go on so. I must be where my life could expand.

It was hard to leave the dear little fellow I had taught to walk and to talk, but I knew he would not be inconsolable. So I only said "I must go," — and turned my back upon the sea, and my face to the banks of the Merrimack.

When I returned I found that I enjoyed even the familiar, unremitting clatter of the mill, because it indicated that something was going on. I liked to feel the people around me, even those whom I did not know, as a wave may like to feel the surrounding waves urging it forward, with or against its own will. I felt that I belonged to the world, that there was something for me to do in it, though I had not yet found out what. Something to do; it might be very little, but still it would be my own work. And then there was the better something which I had almost forgotten, — *to be!* Underneath my dull thoughts the old aspirations were smouldering, the old ideals rose and beckoned to me through the rekindling light.

It was always aspiration rather than ambition by which I felt myself stirred. I did not care to outstrip others, and become what is called "distinguished," were that a possibility, so much as I longed to answer the Voice that invited, ever receding, up to invisible heights, however unattainable they might seem. I was conscious of a desire that others should feel something coming to them out of my life like the breath of flowers, the whisper of the winds, the warmth of the sunshine, and the depth of the sky. That, I felt, did not require great gifts or a fine education. We might all be that to each other. And there was no opportunity for vanity or pride in receiving a beautiful influence, and giving it out again.

I do not suppose that I definitely thought all this, though I find that the verses I wrote for our two mill magazines at about this time often expressed these and similar longings. They were vague, and they were too likely to dissipate themselves in mere dreams. But our aspirations come to us from a source far beyond ourselves. Happy are they who are "not disobedient unto the heavenly vision"!

A girl of sixteen sees the world before her through rose-tinted mists, a blending of celestial colors and earthly exhalations, and she cannot separate their elements, if she would; they all belong to the landscape of her youth. It is the mystery of the meeting horizons, — the visible beauty seeking to lose and find itself in the Invisible.

In returning to my daily toil among workmates from the hill-country, the scenery to which they belonged became also a part of my life. They brought the mountains with them, a new background and a new hope. We shared an uneven path and homely occupations; but above us hung glorious summits never wholly out of sight. Every blossom and every dewdrop at our feet was touched with some tint of that far-off splendor, and every pebble by the wayside was a messenger from the peak that our feet would stand upon by and by.

The true climber knows the delight of trusting his path, of following it without seeing a step before him, or a glimpse of blue sky above him, sometimes only knowing that it is the right path because it is the only one, and because it leads upward. This our daily duty was to us. Though we did not always know it, the faithful plodder was sure to win the heights. Unconsciously we learned the lesson that only by humble Doing can any of us win the lofty possibilities of Being. For indeed, what we all want to find is not so much our place as our path. The path leads to the place, and the place, when we have found it, is only a clearing by the roadside, an opening into another path.

And no comrades are so dear as those who have broken with us a pioneer road which it will be safe and good for others to follow; which will furnish a plain clue for all bewildered travelers hereafter. There is no more exhilarating human experience than this, and perhaps it is the highest angelic one. It may be that some such mutual work is to link us forever with one another in the Infinite Life.

The girls who toiled together at Lowell were clearing away a few weeds from the overgrown track of independent labor for other women. They practically said, by numbering themselves among factory girls, that in our country no real odium could be attached to any honest toil that any self-respecting woman might undertake.

I regard it as one of the privileges of my youth that I was permitted to grow up among those active, interesting girls, whose lives were not mere echoes of other lives, but had principle and purpose distinctly their own. Their vigor of character was a natural development. The New Hampshire girls who came to Lowell were descendants of the sturdy backwoodsmen who settled that State scarcely a hundred years before. Their grandmothers had suffered the hardships of frontier life, had known the horrors of savage warfare when the beautiful valleys of the Connecticut and the Merrimack were threaded with Indian trails from Canada to the white settlements. Those young women did justice to their inheritance. They were earnest and capable; ready to undertake anything that was worth doing. My dreamy, indolent nature was shamed into activity among them. They gave me a larger, firmer ideal of womanhood.

Often during the many summers and autumns that of late years I have spent among the New Hampshire hills, sometimes far up the mountain sides, where I could listen to the first song of the little brooks setting out on their journey to join the very river that flowed at my feet when I was a working-girl on its banks, — the Merrimack, — I have felt as if I could also hear the early music of my workmates' lives, those who were born among these glorious summits. Pure, strong, crystalline natures, carrying down with them the light of blue skies and the freshness of free winds to their place of toil, broadening and strengthening as they went on, who can tell how they have refreshed the world, how beautifully they have blended their being with the great ocean of results? A brook's life is like the life of a maiden. The rivers receive their strength from the rock-born rills, from the unfailing purity of the mountain-streams.

A girl's place in the world is a very strong one: it is a pity that she does not always see it so. It is strongest through her natural impulse to steady herself by leaning upon the Eternal Life, the only Reality; and her weakness comes also from her inclination to lean against something, — upon an unworthy support, rather than none at all. She often lets her life get broken into fragments among the flimsy trellises of fashion and conventionality, when it might be a perfect thing in the upright beauty of its own consecrated freedom.

Yet girlhood seldom appreciates itself. We often hear a girl wishing that she were a boy.

That seems so strange! God made no mistake in her creation. He sent her into the world full of power and will to be a *helper;* and only He knows how much his world needs help. She is here to make this great house of humanity a habitable and a beautiful place, without and within, — a true home for every one of his children. It matters not if she is poor, if she has to toil for her daily bread, or even if she is surrounded by coarseness and uncongeniality: nothing can deprive her of her natural instinct to help, of her birthright as a helper. These very hindrances may, with faith and patience, develop in her a nobler womanhood.

No ; let girls be as thankful that they are girls as that they are human beings ; for they also, according to his own loving plan for them, were created in the image of God. Their real power, the divine dowry of womanhood, is that of receiving and giving inspiration. In this a girl often surpasses her brother; and it is for her to hold firmly and faithfully to her holiest instincts, so that when he lets his standard droop, she may, through her spiritual strength, be a standard-bearer for him. Courage and self-reliance are now held to be virtues as womanly as they are manly ; for the world has grown wise enough to see that nothing except a life can really help another life. It is strange that it should ever have held any other theory about woman.

That was a true use of the word "help" that grew up so naturally in the rendering and receiving of womanly service in the old-fashioned New England household. A girl came into a family as one of the home-group, to share its burdens, to feel that they were her own. The woman who employed her, if her nature was at all generous, could not feel that money alone was an equivalent for a heart's service ; she added to it her friendship, her gratitude and esteem. The domestic problem can never be rightly settled until the old idea of mutual help is in some way restored. This is a question for girls of the present generation to consider, and she who can bring about a practical solution of it will win the world's gratitude.

We used sometimes to see it claimed, in public prints, that it would be better for all of us mill-girls to be working in families, at domestic service, than to be where we were.

Perhaps the difficulties of modern housekeepers did begin with the opening of the Lowell factories. Country girls were naturally independent, and the feeling that at this new work the few hours they had of every-day leisure were entirely their own was a satisfaction to them. They preferred it to going out as " hired help." It was like a young man's pleasure in entering upon business for himself. Girls had never tried that experiment before, and they liked it. It brought out in them a dormant strength of character which the

world did not previously see, but now fully ac-
knowledges. Of course they had a right to con-
tinue at that freer kind of work as long as they
chose, although their doing so increased the perplexities of the housekeeping problem for themselves even, since many of them were to become,
and did become, American house-mistresses.

It would be a step towards the settlement of
this vexed and vexing question if girls would decline to classify each other by their occupations,
which among us are usually only temporary, and
are continually shifting from one pair of hands to
another. Changes of fortune come so abruptly
that the millionaire's daughter of to-day may be
glad to earn her living by sewing or sweeping to-
morrow.

It is the first duty of every woman to recognize the mutual bond of universal womanhood.
Let her ask herself whether she would like to
hear herself or her sister spoken of as a shop-
girl, or a factory-girl, or a servant-girl, if necessity had compelled her for a time to be employed
in either of the ways indicated. If she would
shrink from it a little, then she is a little inhu-
man when she puts her unknown human sisters
who are so occupied into a class by themselves,
feeling herself to be somewhat their superior.
She is really the superior person who has accepted
her work and is doing it faithfully, whatever it is.
This designating others by their casual employ-

ments prevents one from making real distinctions, from knowing persons as persons. A false standard is set up in the minds of those who classify and of those who are classified.

Perhaps it is chiefly the fault of ladies themselves that the word "lady" has nearly lost its original meaning (a noble one) indicating sympathy and service; — bread-giver to those who are in need. The idea that it means something external in dress or circumstances has been too generally adopted by rich and poor; and this, coupled with the sweeping notion that in our country one person is just as good as another, has led to ridiculous results, like that of saleswomen calling themselves "salesladies." I have even heard a chambermaid at a hotel introduce herself to guests as "the chamberlady."

I do not believe that any Lowell mill-girl was ever absurd enough to wish to be known as a "factory-lady," although most of them knew that "factory-girl" did not represent a high type of womanhood in the Old World. But they themselves belonged to the New World, not to the Old; and they were making their own traditions, to hand down to their Republican descendants, — one of which was and is that honest work has no need to assert itself or to humble itself in a nation like ours, but simply to take its place as one of the foundation-stones of the Republic.

The young women who worked at Lowell had

the advantage of living in a community where character alone commanded respect. They never, at their work or away from it, heard themselves contemptuously spoken of on account of their occupation, except by the ignorant or weak-minded, whose comments they were of course too sensible to heed.

We may as well acknowledge that one of the unworthy tendencies of womankind is towards petty estimates of other women. This classifying habit illustrates the fact. If we must classify our sisters, let us broaden ourselves by making large classifications. We might all place ourselves in one of two ranks — the women who do something, and the women who do nothing; the first being of course the only creditable place to occupy. And if we would escape from our pettinesses, as we all may and should, the way to do it is to find the key to other lives, and live in their largeness, by sharing their outlook upon life. Even poorer people's windows will give us a new horizon, and often a far broader one than our own.

X.

MILL-GIRLS' MAGAZINES.

THERE was a passage from Cowper that my
sister used to quote to us, because, she said, she
often repeated it to herself, and found that it did
her good : —

> " In such a world, so thorny, and where none
> Finds happiness unblighted, or if found,
> Without some thistly sorrow at its side,
> It seems the part of wisdom, and no sin
> Against the law of love, to measure lots
> With less distinguished than ourselves, that thus
> We may with patience bear our moderate ills,
> And sympathize with others, suffering more."

I think she made us feel — she certainly made
me feel — that our lot was in many ways an un-
usually fortunate one, and full of responsibilities.
She herself was always thinking what she could
do for others, not only immediately about her, but
in the farthest corners of the earth.   She had her
Sabbath-school class, and visited all the children
in it ; she sat up all night, very often, watching
by a sick girl's bed, in the hospital or in some distant boarding-house ; she gave money to send to
missionaries, or to help build new churches in the
city, when she was earning only eight or ten dol-

lars a month clear of her board, and could afford herself but one "best dress," besides her working clothes. That best dress was often nothing but a Merrimack print. But she insisted that it was a great saving of trouble to have just this one, because she was not obliged to think what she should wear if she were invited out to spend an evening. And she kept track of all the great philanthropic movements of the day. She felt deeply the shame and wrong of American slavery, and tried to make her workmates see and feel it too. (Petitions to Congress for the abolition of slavery in the District of Columbia were circulated nearly every year among the mill-girls, and received thousands of signatures.)

Whenever she was not occupied with her work or her reading, or with looking after us younger ones, — two or three hours a day was all the time she could call her own, — she was sure to be away on some errand of friendliness or mercy.

Those who do most for others are always those who are called upon continually to do a little more, and who find a way to do it. People go to them as to a bank that never fails. And surely, they who have an abundance of life in themselves and who give their life out freely to others are the only really rich.

Two dollars a week sounds very small, but in Emilie's hands it went farther than many a princely fortune of to-day, because she managed with it to make so many people happy. But then she wanted absolutely nothing for herself; nothing but the privilege of helping others.

I seem to be eulogizing my sister, though I am simply relating matters of fact. I could not, however, illustrate my own early experience, except by the lives around me which most influenced mine. And it was true that our smaller and more self-centred natures in touching hers caught something of her spirit, the contagion of her warm heart and healthy energy. For health is more contagious than disease, and lives that exhale sweetness around them from the inner heaven of their souls keep the world wholesome.

I tried to follow her in my faltering way, and was gratified when she would send me to look up one of her stray children, or would let me watch with her at night by a sick-bed. I think it was partly for the sake of keeping as close to her as I could — though not without a sincere desire to consecrate myself to the Best — that I became, at about thirteen, a member of the church which we attended.

Our minister was a scholarly man, of refined tastes and a sensitive organization, fervently spiritual, and earnestly devoted to his work. It was an education to grow up under his influence. I shall never forget the effect left by the tones of his voice when he first spoke to me, a child of ten years, at a neighborhood prayer-meeting in my mother's sitting-room. He had been inviting his listeners to the friendship of Christ, and turning to my little sister and me, he said, —

"And these little children, too; won't they come?"

The words, and his manner of saying them, brought the tears to my eyes. Once only before, far back in my earlier childhood — I have already mentioned the incident — had I heard that Name spoken so tenderly and familiarly, yet so reverently. It was as if he had been gazing into the face of an invisible Friend, and had just turned from Him to look into ours, while he gave us his message, that He loved us.

In that moment I again caught a glimpse of One whom I had always known, but had often forgotten, — One who claimed me as his Father's child, and would never let me go. It was a real Face that I saw, a real Voice that I heard, a real Person who was calling me. I could not mistake the Presence that had so often drawn near me and shone with sunlike eyes into my soul. The words, " Lord, lift Thou up the light of thy countenance upon us! " had always given me the feeling that a beautiful sunrise does. It is indeed a sunrise text, for is not He the Light of the World?

And peaceful sunshine seemed pouring in at the windows of my life on the day when I stood in the aisle before the pulpit with a group, who,

though young, were all much older than myself,
and took with them the vows that bound us to
his service. Of what was then said and read I
scarcely remember more than the words of heavenly welcome in the Epistle, "Now therefore ye
are no more strangers and foreigners." It was
like coming home, like stepping a little farther
beyond the threshold in at the open door of our
Father's house.

Perhaps I was too young to assume those vows.
Had I deferred it a few years there would have
been serious intellectual hindrances. But it was
not the Articles of Faith I was thinking of, although there was a long list of them, to which we
all bowed assent, as was the custom. It was
the home-coming to the "house not made with
hands," the gladness of signifying that I belonged
to God's spiritual family, and was being drawn
closer to his heart, with whom none of us are
held as "strangers and foreigners."

I felt that I was taking up again the clue which
had been put into my childish hand at baptism,
and was being led on by it into the unfolding
mysteries of life. Should I ever let it slip from
me, and lose the way to the "many mansions"
that now seemed so open and so near? I could
not think so. It is well that we cannot foresee
our falterings and failures. At least I could never
forget that I had once felt my own and other lives
bound together with the Eternal Life by an invisible thread.

The vague, fitful desire I had felt from my childhood to be something to the world I lived in, to give it something of the inexpressible sweetness that often seemed pouring through me, I knew not whence, now began to shape itself into a definite outreach towards the Source of all spiritual life. To draw near to the One All-Beautiful Being, Christ, to know Him as our spirits may know The Spirit, to receive the breath of his infinitely loving Life into mine, that I might breathe out that fragrance again into the lives around me, — this was the longing wish that, half hidden from myself, lay deep beneath all other desires of my soul. This was what religion grew to mean to me, what it is still growing to mean, more simply and more clearly as the years go on.

The heart must be very humble to which this heavenly approach is permitted. It knows that it has nothing in itself, nothing for others, which it has not received. The loving Voice of Him who gives his friends his errands to do whispers through them constantly, " Ye are not your own."

There may be those who would think my narrative more entertaining, if I omitted these inner experiences, and related only lighter incidents. But one thing I was aware of, from the time I began to think and to wonder about my own life, — that what I felt and thought was far more real to me than the things that happened.

Circumstances are only the keys that unlock for us the secret of ourselves; and I learned very early that though there is much to enjoy in this beautiful outside world, there is much more to love, to believe in, and to seek, in the invisible world out of which it all grows. What has best revealed our true selves to ourselves must be most helpful to others, and one can willingly sacrifice some natural reserves to such an end. Besides, if we tell our own story at all, we naturally wish to tell the truest part of it.

Work, study, and worship were interblended in our life. The church was really the home-centre to many, perhaps to most of us; and it was one of the mill regulations that everybody should go to church somewhere. There must have been an earnest group of ministers at Lowell, since nearly all the girls attended public worship from choice.

Our minister joined us in our social gatherings, often inviting us to his own house, visiting us at our work, accompanying us on our picnics down the river-bank, — a walk of a mile or so took us into charmingly picturesque scenery, and we always walked, — suggesting books for our reading, and assisting us in our studies.

The two magazines published by the mill-girls, the "Lowell Offering" and the "Operatives' Magazine," originated with literary meetings in the vestry of two religious societies, the first in the Universalist Church, the second in the First

Congregational, to which my sister and I belonged.

On account of our belonging there, our contributions were given to the "Operatives' Magazine," the first periodical for which I ever wrote, issued by the literary society of which our minister took charge. He met us on regular evenings, read aloud our poems and sketches, and made such critical suggestions as he thought desirable. This magazine was edited by two young women, both of whom had been employed in the mills, although at that time they were teachers in the public schools — a change which was often made by mill-girls after a few months' residence at Lowell. A great many of them were district-school teachers at their homes in the summer, spending only the winters at their work.

The two magazines went on side by side for a year or two, and then were united in the "Lowell Offering," which had made the first experiment of the kind by publishing a trial number or two at irregular intervals. My sister had sent some verses of mine, on request, to be published in one of those specimen numbers. But we were not acquainted with the editor of the "Offering," and we knew only a few of its contributors. The Universalist Church, in the vestry of which they met, was in a distant part of the city. Socially, the place where we worshiped was the place where we naturally came together in other ways. The churches were all filled to overflowing, so that the grouping together of the girls by their denominational preferences was almost unavoidable. It was in some such way as this that two magazines were started instead of one. If the girls who enjoyed writing had not been so many and so scattered, they might have made the better arrangement of joining their forces from the beginning.

I was too young a contributor to be at first of much value to either periodical. They began their regular issues, I think, while I was the nursemaid of my little nephews at Beverly. When I returned to Lowell, at about sixteen, I found my sister Emilie interested in the " Operatives' Magazine," and we both contributed to it regularly, until it was merged in the " Lowell Offering," to which we then transferred our writing-efforts. It did not occur to us to call these efforts " literary." I know that I wrote just as I did for our little " Diving Bell," — as a sort of pastime, and because my daily toil was mechanical, and furnished no occupation for my thoughts. Perhaps the fact that most of us wrote in this way accounted for the rather sketchy and fragmentary character of our " Magazine." It gave evidence that we thought, and that we thought upon solid and serious matters ; but the criticism of one of our superintendents upon it, very kindly given, was undoubtedly just : " It has plenty of pith, but it lacks point."

The "Offering" had always more of the literary spirit and touch. It was, indeed, for the first two years, edited by a gentleman of acknowledged literary ability. But people seemed to be more interested in it after it passed entirely into the hands of the girls themselves.

The "Operatives' Magazine" had a decidedly religious tone. We who wrote for it were loyal to our Puritanic antecedents, and considered it all-important that our lightest actions should be moved by some earnest impulse from behind. We might write playfully, but there must be conscience and reverence somewhere within it all. We had been taught, and we believed, that idle words were a sin, whether spoken or written. This, no doubt, gave us a gravity of expression rather unnatural to youth.

In looking over the bound volume of this magazine, I am amused at the grown-up style of thought assumed by myself, probably its very youngest contributor. I wrote a dissertation on "Fame," quoting from Pollok, Cowper, and Milton, and ending with Diedrich Knickerbocker's definition of immortal fame, — "Half a page of dirty paper." For other titles I had " Thoughts on Beauty; " " Gentility ; " " Sympathy," etc. And in one longish poem, entitled " My Childhood " (written when I was about fifteen), I find verses like these, which would seem to have come out of a mature experience : —

My childhood ! O those pleasant days, when everything seemed
    free,
And in the broad and verdant fields I frolicked merrily ;
When joy came to my bounding heart with every wild bird's
    song,
And Nature's music in my ears was ringing all day long !

  .   .   .   .

And yet I would not call them back, those blessed times of
    yore,
For riper years are fraught with joys I dreamed not of before.
The labyrinth of Science opes with wonders every day ;
And friendship hath full many a flower to cheer life's dreary
    way.

And glancing through the pages of the "Lowell Offering" a year or two later, I see that I
continued to dismalize myself at times, quite un-
necessarily. The title of one string of morbid
verses is "The Complaint of a Nobody," in which
I compare myself to a weed growing up in a garden; and the conclusion of it all is this stanza: —

    When the fierce storms are raging, I will not repine,
      Though I 'm heedlessly crushed in the strife ;
    For surely 't were better oblivion were mine
      Than a worthless, inglorious life.

Now I do not suppose that I really considered
myself a weed, though I did sometimes fancy that
a different kind of cultivation would tend to make
me a more useful plant. I am glad to remember
that these discontented fits were only occasional,
for certainly they were unreasonable. I was not
unhappy ; this was an affectation of unhappiness ;
and half conscious that it was, I hid it behind a
different signature from my usual one.

How truly Wordsworth describes this phase of undeveloped feeling : —

> " In youth sad fancies we affect,
> In luxury of disrespect
> To our own prodigal excess
> Of too familiar happiness."

It is a very youthful weakness to exaggerate passing moods into deep experiences, and if we put them down on paper, we get a fine opportunity of laughing at ourselves, if we live to outgrow them, as most of us do. I think I must have had a frequent fancy that I was not long for this world. Perhaps I thought an early death rather picturesque; many young people do. There is a certain kind of poetry that fosters this idea; that delights in imaginary youthful victims, and has, reciprocally, its youthful devotees. One of my blank verse poems in the " Offering " is entitled " The Early Doomed." It begins, —

> And must I die ? The world is bright to me,
> And everything that looks upon me, smiles.

Another poem is headed " Memento Mori ; " and another, entitled a " Song in June," which ought to be cheerful, goes off into the doleful request to somebody, or anybody, to

> Weave me a shroud in the month of June !

I was, perhaps, healthier than the average girl, and had no predisposition to a premature decline ; and in reviewing these absurdities of my pen, I feel like saying to any young girl who inclines to

rhyme, " Don't sentimentalize ! Write more of
what you see than of what you feel, and let your
feelings realize themselves to others in the shape of
worthy actions. Then they will be natural, and
will furnish you with something worth writing."

It is fair to myself to explain, however, that
many of these verses of mine were written chiefly
as exercises in rhythmic expression. I remember
this distinctly about one of my poems with a terrible title, — " The Murderer's Request," — in
which I made an imaginary criminal pose for me,
telling where he would not and where he would
like to be buried. I modeled my verses, —

> Bury ye me on some storm-rifted mountain,
> O'erhanging the depths of a yawning abyss, —

upon Byron's, —

> " Know ye the land where the cypress and myrtle
> Are emblems of deeds that are done in their clime ; "

and I was only trying to see how near I could approach to his exquisite metre. I do not think I
felt at all murderous in writing it ; but a more
innocent subject would have been in better taste,
and would have met the exigencies of the dactyl
quite as well.

It is also only fair to myself to say that my
rhyming was usually of a more wholesome kind.
I loved Nature as I knew her, — in our stern,
blustering, stimulating New England, — and I
chanted the praises of Winter, of snow-storms, and

of March winds (I always took pride in my birth
month, March), with hearty delight.

Flowers had begun to bring me messages from
their own world when I was a very small child,
and they never withdrew their companionship
from my thoughts, for there came summers when
I could only look out of the mill window and
dream about them.

I had one pet window plant of my own, a red
rose-bush, almost a perpetual bloomer, that I kept
beside me at my work for years. I parted with
it only when I went away to the West, and then
with regret, for it had been to me like a human
little friend. But the wild flowers had my heart.
I lived and breathed with them, out under the
free winds of heaven; and when I could not see
them, I wrote about them. Much that I contributed to those mill-magazine pages, they suggested,
— my mute teachers, comforters, and inspirers.
It seems to me that any one who does not care for
wild flowers misses half the sweetness of this
mortal life.

Horace Smith's " Hymn to the Flowers " was a
continual delight to me, after I made its acquaintance. It seemed as if all the wild blossoms of the
woods had wandered in and were twining themselves around the whirring spindles, as I repeated
it, verse after verse. Better still, they drew me
out, in fancy, to their own forest-haunts under
" cloistered boughs," where each swinging " flo-

ral bell" was ringing "a call to prayer," and making "Sabbath in the fields."

Bryant's "Forest Hymn" did me an equally beautiful service. I knew every word of it. It seemed to me that Bryant understood the very heart and soul of the flowers as hardly anybody else did. He made me feel as if they were really related to us human beings. In fancy my feet pressed the turf where they grew, and I knew them as my little sisters, while my thoughts touched them, one by one, saying with him, —

> "That delicate forest-flower,
> With scented breath, and look so like a smile,
> Seems, as it issues from the shapeless mould,
> An emanation of the indwelling Life,
> A visible token of the upholding Love,
> That are the soul of this wide universe."

I suppose that most of my readers will scarcely be older than I was when I wrote my sermonish little poems under the inspiration of the flowers at my factory work, and perhaps they will be interested in reading a specimen or two from the "Lowell Offering:" —

LIVE LIKE THE FLOWERS.

> Cheerfully wave they o'er valley and mountain,
> Gladden the desert, and smile by the fountain;
> Pale discontent in no young blossom lowers : —
> Live like the flowers!

> Meekly their buds in the heavy rain bending,
> Softly their hues with the mellow light blending,
> Gratefully welcoming sunlight and showers : —
> Live like the flowers!

Freely their sweets on the wild breezes flinging,
While in their depths are new odors upspringing : —
(Blessedness twofold of Love's holy dowers,)
Live like the flowers !

Gladly they heed Who their brightness has given:
Blooming on earth, look they all up to heaven ;
Humbly look up from their loveliest bowers : —
Live like the flowers !

Peacefully droop they when autumn is sighing ;
Breathing mild fragrance around them in dying,
Sleep they in hope of Spring's freshening hours : —
Die like the flowers !

The prose-poem that follows was put into a rhymed version by several unknown hands in periodicals of that day, so that at last I also wrote one, in self-defense, to claim my own waif. But it was a prose-poem that I intended it to be, and I think it is better so.

" BRING BACK MY FLOWERS."

On the bank of a rivulet sat a rosy child. Her lap was filled with flowers, and a garland of rose-buds was twined around her neck. Her face was as radiant as the sunshine that fell upon it, and her voice was as clear as that of the bird which warbled at her side.

The little stream went singing on, and with every gush of its music the child lifted a flower in her dimpled hand, and, with a merry laugh, threw it upon the water. In her glee she forgot that her treasures were growing less, and with the swift motion of childhood, she flung them upon the sparkling tide, until every bud and blossom had disappeared.

Then, seeing her loss, she sprang to her feet, and bursting into tears, called aloud to the stream, "Bring back my flowers!" But the stream danced along, regardless of her sorrow; and as it bore the blooming burden away, her words came back in a taunting echo, along its reedy margin. And long after, amid the wailing of the breeze and the fitful bursts of childish grief, was heard the fruitless cry, "Bring back my flowers!"

Merry maiden, who art idly wasting the precious moments so bountifully bestowed upon thee, see in the thoughtless child an emblem of thyself! Each moment is a perfumed flower. Let its fragrance be diffused in blessings around thee, and ascend as sweet incense to the beneficent Giver!

Else, when thou hast carelessly flung them from thee, and seest them receding on the swift waters of Time, thou wilt cry, in tones more sorrowful than those of the weeping child, "Bring back my flowers!" And thy only answer will be an echo from the shadowy Past, — "Bring back my flowers!"

In the above, a reminiscence of my German studies comes back to me. I was an admirer of Jean Paul, and one of my earliest attempts at translation was his "New Year's Night of an Unhappy Man," with its yet haunting glimpse of "a fair long paradise beyond the mountains." I am not sure but the idea of trying my hand at a "prose-poem" came to me from Richter, though it may have been from Herder or Krummacher, whom I also enjoyed and attempted to translate.

I have a manuscript-book still, filled with these youthful efforts. I even undertook to put German verse into English verse, not wincing at the greatest — Goethe and Schiller. These studies were pursued in the pleasant days of cloth-room leisure, when my work claimed me only seven or eight hours in a day.

I suppose I should have tried to write, — perhaps I could not very well have helped attempting it, — under any circumstances. My early efforts would not, probably, have found their way into print, however, but for the coincident publication of the two mill-girls' magazines, just as I entered my teens. I fancy that almost everything any of us offered them was published, though I never was let in to editorial secrets. The editors of both magazines were my seniors, and I felt greatly honored by their approval of my contributions.

One of the " Offering " editors was a Unitarian clergyman's daughter, and had received an excellent education. The other was a remarkably brilliant and original young woman, who wrote novels that were published by the Harpers of New York while she was employed at Lowell. The two had rooms together for a time, where the members of the "Improvement Circle," chiefly composed of " Offering " writers, were hospitably received.

The " Operatives' Magazine " and the " Lowell Offering" were united in the year 1842, under the title of the " Lowell Offering and Magazine."

(And — to correct a mistake which has crept into print — I will say that I never attained the honor of being editor of either of these magazines. I was only one of their youngest contributors. The " Lowell Offering" closed its existence when I was a little more than twenty years old. The only continuous editing I have ever been engaged in was upon " Our Young Folks." About twenty years ago I was editor-in-charge of that magazine for a year or more, and I had previously been its assistant-editor from its beginning. These explanatory items, however, do not quite belong to my narrative, and I return to our magazines.)

We did not receive much criticism; perhaps it would have been better for us if we had. But then we did not set ourselves up to be literary; though we enjoyed the freedom of writing what we pleased, and seeing how it looked in print. It was good practice for us, and that was all that we desired. We were complimented and quoted. When a Philadelphia paper copied one of my little poems, suggesting some verbal improvements, and predicting recognition for me in the future, I felt for the first time that there might be such a thing as public opinion worth caring for, in addition to doing one's best for its own sake.

Fame, indeed, never had much attraction for me, except as it took the form of friendly recognition and the sympathetic approval of worthy

judges. I wished to do good and true things, but
not such as would subject me to the stare of coldly
curious eyes. I could never imagine a girl feeling any pleasure in placing herself "before the
public." The privilege of seclusion must be the
last one a woman can willingly sacrifice.

And, indeed, what we wrote was not remarkable, — perhaps no more so than the usual school
compositions of intelligent girls. It would hardly
be worth while to refer to it particularly, had
not the Lowell girls and their magazines been so
frequently spoken of as something phenomenal.
But it was a perfectly natural outgrowth of those
girls' previous life. For what were we? Girls
who were working in a factory for the time, to be
sure; but none of us had the least idea of con-
tinuing at that kind of work permanently. Our
composite photograph, had it been taken, would
have been the representative New England girlhood of those days. We had all been fairly educated at public or private schools, and many
of us were resolutely bent upon obtaining a better
education. Very few were among us without some
distinct plan for bettering the condition of themselves and those they loved. For the first time,
our young women had come forth from their home
retirement in a throng, each with her own individual purpose. For twenty years or so, Lowell
might have been looked upon as a rather select in-
dustrial school for young people. The girls there

were just such girls as are knocking at the doors
of young women's colleges to-day. They had
come to work with their hands, but they could not
hinder the working of their minds also. Their
mental activity was overflowing at every possible
outlet.

Many of them were supporting themselves at
schools like Bradford Academy or Ipswich Seminary half the year, by working in the mills the
other half. Mount Holyoke Seminary broke upon
the thoughts of many of them as a vision of hope,
— I remember being dazzled by it myself for a
while, — and Mary Lyon's name was honored no-
where more than among the Lowell mill-girls.
Meanwhile they were improving themselves and
preparing for their future in every possible way,
by purchasing and reading standard books, by attending lectures and evening classes of their own
getting up, and by meeting each other for reading
and conversation.

That they should write was no more strange
than that they should study, or read, or think.
And yet there were those to whom it seemed in-
credible that a girl could, in the pauses of her
work, put together words with her pen that it
would do to print; and after a while the asser-
tion was circulated, through some distant newspaper, that our magazine was not written by ourselves at all, but by "Lowell lawyers." This
seemed almost too foolish a suggestion to contra-

dict, but the editor of the " Offering " thought it best to give the name and occupation of some of the writers by way of refutation. It was for this reason (much against my own wish) that my real name was first attached to anything I wrote. I was then book-keeper in the cloth-room of the Lawrence Mills. We had all used any fanciful signature we chose, varying it as we pleased. After I began to read and love Wordsworth, my favorite *nom de plume* was " Rotha." In the later numbers of the magazine, the editor more frequently made use of my initials. One day I was surprised by seeing my name in full in Griswold's " Female Poets; " — no great distinction, however, since there were a hundred names or so, besides.

It has seemed necessary to give these gossip items about myself; but the real interest of every separate life-story is involved in the larger life-history which is going on around it. We do not know ourselves without our companions and surroundings. I cannot narrate my workmates' separate experiences, but I know that because of having lived among them, and because of having felt the beauty and power of their lives, I am different from what I should otherwise have been, and it is my own fault if I am not better for my life with them.

In recalling those years of my girlhood at Lowell, I often think that I knew then what real society is better perhaps than ever since. For in

that large gathering together of young womanhood there were many choice natures — some of
the choicest in all our excellent New England,
and there were no false social standards to hold
them apart. It is the best society when people
meet sincerely, on the ground of their deepest
sympathies and highest aspirations, without conventionality or cliques or affectation; and it was
in that way that these young girls met and became
acquainted with each other, almost of necessity.

There were all varieties of woman-nature among
them, all degrees of refinement and cultivation,
and, of course, many sharp contrasts of agreeable
and disagreeable. It was not always the most
cultivated, however, who were the most compan-
ionable. There were gentle, untaught girls, as
fresh and simple as wild flowers, whose unpre-
tending goodness of heart was better to have than
bookishness; girls who loved everybody, and were
loved by everybody. Those are the girls that I
remember best, and their memory is sweet as a
breeze from the clover fields.

As I recall the throngs of unknown girlish
forms that used to pass and repass me on the familiar road to the mill-gates, and also the few
that I knew so well, those with whom I worked,
thought, read, wrote, studied, and worshiped, my
thoughts send a heartfelt greeting to them all,
wherever in God's beautiful, busy universe they
may now be scattered : —

"I am glad I have lived in the world with you!"

XI

READING AND STUDYING.

MY return to mill-work involved making acquaintance with a new kind of machinery. The spinning-room was the only one I had hitherto known anything about. Now my sister Emilie found a place for me in the dressing-room, beside herself. It was more airy, and fewer girls were in the room, for the dressing-frame itself was a large, clumsy affair, that occupied a great deal of space. Mine seemed to me as unmanageable as an overgrown spoilt child. It had to be watched in a dozen directions every minute, and even then it was always getting itself and me into trouble. I felt as if the half-live creature, with its great, groaning joints and whizzing fan, was aware of my incapacity to manage it, and had a fiendish spite against me. I contracted an unconquerable dislike to it; indeed, I had never liked, and never could learn to like, any kind of machinery. And this machine finally conquered me. It was humiliating, but I had to acknowledge that there were some things I could not do, and I retired from the field, vanquished.

The two things I had enjoyed in this room

were that my sister was with me, and that our
windows looked toward the west. When the work
was running smoothly, we looked out together and
quoted to each other all the sunset-poetry we
could remember. Our tastes did not quite agree.
Her favorite description of the clouds was from
Pollok : —

> " They seemed like chariots of saints,
> By fiery coursers drawn; as brightly hued
> As if the glorious, bushy, golden locks
> Of thousand cherubim had been shorn off,
> And on the temples hung of morn and even."

I liked better a translation from the German,
beginning

> "Methinks it were no pain to die
> On such an eve, while such a sky
> O'ercanopies the west."

And she generally had to hear the whole poem,
for I was very fond of it; though the especial
verse that I contrasted with hers was, —

> " There's peace and welcome in yon sea
> Of endless blue tranquillity;
> Those clouds are living things;
> I trace their veins of liquid gold,
> And see them silently unfold
> Their soft and fleecy wings."

Then she would tell me that my nature inclined to quietness and harmony, while hers asked
for motion and splendor. I wondered whether it
really were so. But that huge, creaking frame-
work beside us would continually intrude upon

our meditations and break up our discussions, and silence all poetry for us with its dull prose.

Emilie found more profitable work elsewhere, and I found some that was less so, but far more satisfactory, as it would give me the openings of leisure which I craved.

The paymaster asked, when I left, "Going where you can earn more money?"

"No," I answered, "I am going where I can have more time."

"Ah, yes!" he said sententiously, "time is money." But that was not my thought about it. "Time is education," I said to myself; for that was what I meant it should be to me.

Perhaps I never gave the wage-earning element in work its due weight. It always seemed to me that the Apostle's idea about worldly possessions was the only sensible one, —

"Having food and raiment, let us be therewith content."

If I could earn enough to furnish that, and have time to study besides, — of course we always gave away a little, however little we had, — it seemed to me a sufficiency. At this time I was receiving two dollars a week, besides my board. Those who were earning much more, and were carefully "laying it up," did not appear to be any happier than I was.

I never thought that the possession of money would make me feel rich: it often does seem to have an opposite effect. But then, I have never had the opportunity of knowing, by experience, how it does make one feel. It is something to have been spared the responsibility of taking charge of the Lord's silver and gold. Let us be thankful for what we have not, as well as for what we have!

Freedom to live one's life truly is surely more desirable than any earthly acquisition or possession; and at my new work I had hours of freedom every day. I never went back again to the bondage of machinery and a working-day thirteen hours long.

The daughter of one of our neighbors, who also went to the same church with us, told me of a vacant place in the cloth-room, where she was, which I gladly secured. This was a low brick building next the counting-room, and a little apart from the mills, where the cloth was folded, stamped, and baled for the market.

There were only half a dozen girls of us, who measured the cloth, and kept an account of the pieces baled, and their length in yards. It pleased me much to have something to do which required the use of pen and ink, and I think there must be a good many scraps of verse buried among the blank pages of those old account-books of mine, that found their way there during the frequent half-hours of waiting for the cloth to be brought in from the mills.

The only machinery in the room was a hydraulic arrangement for pressing the cloth into bales, managed by two or three men, one of whom was quite a poet, and a fine singer also. His hymns were frequently in request, on public occasions. He lent me the first volume of Whittier's poems that I ever saw. It was a small book, containing mostly Antislavery pieces. "The Yankee Girl" was one of them, fully to appreciate the spirit of which, it is necessary to have been a working-girl in slave-labor times. New England Womanhood crowned Whittier as her laureate from the day of his heroine's spirited response to the slaveholder : —

> "O, could ye have seen her — that pride of our girls —
> Arise and cast back the dark wealth of her curls,
> With a scorn in her eye that the gazer could feel,
> And a glance like the sunshine that flashes on steel!
>
> "'Go back, haughty Southron! Go back! for thy gold
> Is red with the blood of the hearts thou hast sold!'"

There was in this volume another poem which is not in any of the later editions, the impression of which, as it remains to me in broken snatches, is very beautiful. It began with the lines

> "Bind up thy tresses, thou beautiful one,
> Of brown in the shadow, and gold in the sun."

It was a refreshment and an inspiration to look into this book between my long rows of figures, and read such poems as "The Angel of Patience," "Follen," "Raphael," and that won-

derfully rendered " Hymn " from Lamartine, that
used to whisper itself through me after I had
read it, like the echo of a spirit's voice : —

> " When the Breath Divine is flowing,
> Zephyr-like o'er all things going,
> And, as the touch of viewless fingers,
> Softly on my soul it lingers,
> Open to a breath the lightest,
> Conscious of a touch the slightest, —
> . . . .
> Then, O Father, Thou alone,
> From the shadow of thy throne,
> To the sighing of my breast
> And its rapture answerest."

I grew so familiar with this volume that I felt
acquainted with the poet long before I met
him. It remained in my desk-drawer for months.
I thought it belonged to my poetic friend, the
baler of cloth. But one day he informed me
that it was a borrowed book; he thought, however, he should claim it for his own, *now that he
had kept it so long.* Upon which remark I delivered it up to the custody of his own conscience,
and saw it no more.

One day, towards the last of my stay at Lowell
(I never changed my work-room again), this same
friendly fellow-toiler handed me a poem to read,
which some one had sent in to us from the counting-room, with the penciled comment, " Singularly beautiful." It was Poe's " Raven," which
had just made its first appearance in some magazine. It seemed like an apparition in literature,

indeed; the sensation it created among the staid, measured lyrics of that day, with its flit of spectral wings, and its ghostly refrain of "Nevermore!" was very noticeable. Poe came to Lowell to live awhile, but it was after I had gone away.

Our national poetry was at this time just beginning to be well known and appreciated. Bryant had published two volumes, and every school child was familiar with his "Death of the Flowers" and "God's First Temples." Some one lent me the "Voices of the Night," the only collection of Longfellow's verse then issued, I think. The "Footsteps of Angels" glided at once into my memory, and took possession of a permanent place there, with its tender melody. "The Last Leaf" and "Old Ironsides" were favorites with everybody who read poetry at all, but I do not think we Lowell girls had a volume of Dr. Holmes's poems at that time.

"The Lady's Book" and "Graham's Magazine" were then the popular periodicals, and the mill-girls took them. I remember that the "nuggets" I used to pick out of one or the other of them when I was quite a child were labeled with the signature of *Harriet E. Beecher*. "Father Morris," and "Uncle Tim," and others of the delightful "May-Flower" sketches first appeared in this way. Irving's "Sketch-Book" all reading people were supposed to have read, and I recall the pleasure it was to me when one of my sisters came into possession of " Knickerbocker's History of New York." It was the first humorous book, as well as the first history, that I ever cared about. And I was pleased enough — for I was a little girl when my fondness for it began — to hear our minister say that he always read Diedrich Knickerbocker for his tired Monday's recreation.

We were allowed to have books in the clothroom. The absence of machinery permitted that privilege. Our superintendent, who was a man of culture and a Christian gentleman of the Puritan-school, dignified and reserved, used often to stop at my desk in his daily round to see what book I was reading. One day it was Mather's " Magnalia," which I had brought from the public library, with a desire to know something of the early history of New England. He looked a little surprised at the archæological turn my mind had taken, but his only comment was, " A valuable old book that." It was a satisfaction to have a superintendent like him, whose granite principles, emphasized by his stately figure and bearing, made him a tower of strength in the church and in the community. He kept a silent, kindly, rigid watch over the corporation-life of which he was the head ; and only those of us who were incidentally admitted to his confidence knew how carefully we were guarded.

We had occasional glimpses into his own well-

ordered home-life, at social gatherings. His little
daughter was in my infant Sabbath-school class
from her fourth to her seventh or eighth year.
She sometimes visited me at my work, and we had
our frolics among the heaps of cloth, as if we
were both children. She had also the same love
of hymns that I had as a child, and she would sit
by my side and repeat to me one after another
that she had learned, not as a task, but because
of her delight in them. One of my sincerest
griefs in going off to the West was that I should
see my little pupil Mary as a child no more.
When I came back, she was a grown-up young
woman.

My friend Anna, who had procured for me the
place and work beside her which I liked so much,
was not at all a bookish person, but we had perhaps a better time together than if she had been.
She was one who found the happiness of her life
in doing kindnesses for others, and in helping
them bear their burdens. Family reverses had
brought her, with her mother and sisters, to Lowell, and this was one strong point of sympathy
between my own family and hers. It was, indeed,
a bond of neighborly union between a great many
households in the young manufacturing city.
Anna's manners and language were those of a
lady, though she had come from the wilds of
Maine, somewhere in the vicinity of Mount Des-
ert, the very name of which seemed in those days

to carry one into a wilderness of mountains and waves. We chatted together at our work on all manner of subjects, and once she astonished me by saying confidentially, in a low tone, " Do you know, I am thirty years old! " She spoke as if she thought the fact implied something serious. My surprise was that she should have taken me into her intimate friendship when I was only seventeen. I should hardly have supposed her older than myself, if she had not volunteered the information.

When I lifted my eyes from her tall, thin figure to her fair face and somewhat sad blue eyes, I saw that she looked a little worn; but I knew that it was from care for others, strangers as well as her own relatives; and it seemed to me as if those thirty loving years were her rose-garland. I became more attached to her than ever.

What a foolish dread it is, — showing unripeness rather than youth, — the dread of growing old! For how can a life be beautified more than by its beautiful years? A living, loving, growing *spirit* can never be old. Emerson says: —

> " Spring still makes spring in the mind,
> When sixty years are told ; "

and some of us are thankful to have lived long enough to bear witness with him to that truth.

The few others who measured cloth with us were nice, bright girls, and some of them remarkably pretty. Our work and the room itself were so clean that in summer we could wear fresh muslin dresses, sometimes white ones, without fear of soiling them. This slight difference of apparel and our fewer work-hours seemed to give us a slight advantage over the toilers in the mills opposite, and we occasionally heard ourselves spoken of as " the cloth-room aristocracy." But that was only in fun. Most of us had served an apprenticeship in the mills, and many of our best friends were still there, preferring their work because it brought them more money than we could earn.

For myself, no amount of money would have been a temptation, compared with my precious daytime freedom. Whole hours of sunshine for reading, for walking, for studying, for writing, for anything that I wanted to do! The days were so lovely and so long! and yet how fast they slipped away! I had not given up my dream of a better education, and as I could not go to school, I began to study by myself.

I had received a pretty thorough drill in the common English branches at the grammar school, and at my employment I only needed a little simple arithmetic. A few of my friends were studying algebra in an evening class, but I had no fancy for mathematics. My first wish was to learn about English Literature, to go back to its very beginnings. It was not then studied even in the higher schools, and I knew no one who could give me any assistance in it, as a teacher.

" Percy's Reliques " and " Chambers' Cyclopædia
of English Literature" were in the city library,
and I used them, making extracts from Chaucer
and Spenser, to fix their peculiarities in my memory, though there was only a taste of them to be
had from the Cyclopædia.

Shakespeare I had read from childhood, in a
fragmentary way. " The Tempest," and " Midsummer Night's Dream," and " King Lear," I
had swallowed among my fairy tales. Now I discovered that the historical plays, notably " Julius
Cæsar " and " Coriolanus," had no less attraction
for me, though of a different kind. But it was
easy for me to forget that I was trying to be a literary student, and slip off from Belmont to Ven-
ice with Portia to witness the discomfiture of
Shylock ; although I did pity the miserable Jew,
and thought he might at least have been allowed
the comfort of his paltry ducats. I do not think
that any of my studying at this time was very
severe ; it was pleasure rather than toil, for I
undertook only the tasks I liked. But what I
learned remained with me, nevertheless.

With Milton I was more familiar than with
any other poet, and from thirteen years of age to
eighteen he was my preference. My friend Angeline and I (another of my cloth-room associates)
made the " Paradise Lost " a language-study in an
evening class, under one of the grammar school
masters, and I never open to the majestic lines, —

" High on a throne of royal state, which far
    Outshone the wealth of Ormus and of Ind,
    Or where the gorgeous east with richest hand
    Showers on her kings barbaric pearl and gold,'' —

without seeing Angeline's kindly, homely face outlined through that magnificence, instead of the
lineaments of the evil angel

" by merit raised
    To that bad eminence.''

She, too, was much older than I, and a most excellent, energetic, and studious young woman. I
wonder if she remembers how hard we tried to get

" Beelzebub — than whom,
    Satan except, none higher sat,''

into the limits of our grammatical rules, — not
altogether with success, I believe.

I copied passages from Jeremy Taylor and the
old theologians into my note-books, and have
found them useful even recently, in preparing
compilations. Dryden and the eighteenth century
poets generally did not interest me, though I tried
to read them from a sense of duty. Pope was an
exception, however. Aphorisms from the " Essay
on Man " were in as common use among us as
those from the Book of Proverbs.

Some of my choicest extracts were in the first
volume of collected poetry I ever owned, a little
red morocco book called " The Young Man's Book
of Poetry.'' It was given me by one of my sisters
when I was about a dozen years old, who rather

apologized for the young man on the title-page, saying that the poetry was just as good as if he were not there.

And, indeed, no young man could have valued it more than I did. It contained selections from standard poets, and choice ones from less familiar sources. One of the extracts was Wordsworth's "Sunset among the Mountains," from the "Excursion," to read which, however often, always lifted me into an ecstasy. That red morocco book was my treasure. It traveled with me to the West, and I meant to keep it as long as I lived. But alas! it was borrowed by a little girl out on the Illinois prairies, who never brought it back. I do not know that I have ever quite forgiven her. I have wished I could look into it again, often and often through the years. But perhaps I ought to be grateful to that little girl for teaching me to be careful about returning borrowed books myself. Only a lover of them can appreciate the loss of one which has been a possession from childhood.

Young and Cowper were considered religious reading, and as such I had always known something of them. The songs of Burns were in the air. Through him I best learned to know poetry as song. I think that I heard the "Cotter's Saturday Night" and "A man's a man for a' that" more frequently quoted than any other poems familiar to my girlhood.

Some of my work-folk acquaintances were regular subscribers to "Blackwood's Magazine" and the "Westminster" and "Edinburgh" reviews, and they lent them to me. These, and Macaulay's "Essays," were a great help and delight. I had also the reading of the "Bibliotheca Sacra" and the "New Englander;" and sometimes of the "North American Review."

By the time I had come down to Wordsworth and Coleridge in my readings of English poetry, I was enjoying it all so much that I could not any longer call it study.

A gift from a friend of Griswold's "Poets and Poetry of England" gave me my first knowledge of Tennyson. It was a great experience to read "Locksley Hall" for the first time while it was yet a new poem, and while one's own young life was stirred by the prophetic spirit of the age that gave it birth.

I had a friend about my own age, and between us there was something very much like what is called a "school-girl friendship," a kind of intimacy supposed to be superficial, but often as deep and permanent as it is pleasant.

Eliza and I managed to see each other every day; we exchanged confidences, laughed and cried together, read, wrote, walked, visited, and studied together. Her dress always had an airy touch which I admired, although I was rather indifferent as to what I wore myself. But she would endeavor to "fix me up" tastefully, while I would

help her to put her compositions for the " Offering" into proper style. She had not begun to go
to school at two years old, repeating the same
routine of study every year of her childhood, as I
had. When a child, I should have thought it almost as much of a disgrace to spell a word wrong,
or make a mistake in the multiplication table, as
to break one of the Ten Commandments. I was
astonished to find that Eliza and other friends
had not been as particularly dealt with in their
early education. But she knew her deficiencies,
and earned money enough to leave her work and
attend a day-school part of the year.

She was an ambitious scholar, and she per-
suaded me into studying the German language
with her. A native professor had formed a class
among young women connected with the mills,
and we joined it. We met, six or eight of us,
at the home of two of these young women, — a
factory boarding-house, — in a neat little parlor
which contained a piano. The professor was a
music-teacher also, and he sometimes brought his
guitar, and let us finish our recitation with a con-
cert. More frequently he gave us the songs of
Deutschland that we begged for. He sang the
" Erl-King ", in his own tongue admirably. We
went through Follen's German Grammar and
Reader : — what a choice collection of extracts
that " Reader " was! We conquered the difficult
gutturals, like those in the numeral " *acht und*

achtzig" (the test of our pronouncing abilities) so completely that the professor told us a native really would understand us! At his request, I put some little German songs into English, which he published as sheet-music, with my name. To hear my words sung quite gave me the feeling of a successful translator. The professor had his own distinctive name for each of his pupils. Eliza was "Naïveté," from her artless manners; and me he called "Etheria," probably on account of my star-gazing and verse-writing habits. Certainly there was never anything ethereal in my visible presence.

A botany class was formed in town by a literary lady who was preparing a school text-book on the subject, and Eliza and I joined that also. The most I recall about that is the delightful flower-hunting rambles we took together. The Linnæan system, then in use, did not give us a very satisfactory key to the science. But we made the acquaintance of hitherto unfamiliar wild flowers that grew around us, and that was the opening to us of another door towards the Beautiful.

Our minister offered to instruct the young people of his parish in ethics, and my sister Emilie and myself were among his pupils. We came to regard Wayland's "Moral Science" (our text-book) as most interesting reading, and it furnished us with many subjects for thought and for social discussion.

Carlyle's " Hero-Worship " brought us a startling and keen enjoyment. It was lent me by a
Dartmouth College student, the brother of one of
my room-mates, soon after it was first published
in this country. The young man did not seem to
know exactly what to think of it, and wanted
another reader's opinion. Few persons could
have welcomed those early writings of Carlyle
more enthusiastically than some of us working-
girls did. The very ruggedness of the sentences
had a fascination for us, like that of climbing
over loose bowlders in a mountain scramble to
get sight of a wonderful landscape.

My room-mate, the student's sister, was the
possessor of an electrifying new poem, — " Festus," — that we sat up nights to read. It does
not seem as if it could be more than forty years
since Sarah and I looked up into each other's
face from the page as the lamplight grew dim,
and said, quoting from the poem, —

" Who can mistake great thoughts ? "

She gave me the volume afterwards, when we went
West together, and I have it still. Its questions
and conjectures were like a glimpse into the chaos
of our own dimly developing inner life. The
fascination of " Festus " was that of wonder,
doubt, and dissent, with great outbursts of an
overmastering faith sweeping over our minds as

we read. Some of our friends thought it not quite safe reading; but we remember it as one of the inspirations of our workaday youth.

We read books, also, that bore directly upon the condition of humanity in our time. "The Glory and Shame of England" was one of them, and it stirred us with a wonderful and painful interest.

We followed travelers and explorers, — Layard to Nineveh, and Stephens to Yucatan. And we were as fond of good story-books as any girls that live in these days of overflowing libraries. One book, a character - picture from history, had a wide popularity in those days. It is a pity that it should be unfamiliar to modern girlhood, — Ware's "Zenobia." The Queen of Palmyra walked among us, and held a lofty place among our ideals of heroic womanhood, never yet obliterated from admiring remembrance.

We had the delight of reading Frederika Bremer's "Home" and "Neighbors" when they were fresh from the fountains of her own heart; and some of us must not be blamed for feeling as if no tales of domestic life half so charming have been written since. Perhaps it is partly because the home-life of Sweden is in itself so delightfully unique.

We read George Borrow's "Bible in Spain," and wandered with him among the gypsies to whom

he seemed to belong. I have never forgotten a
verse that this strange traveler picked up somewhere among the Zincali : —

> " I 'll joyfully labor, both night and day,
>   To aid my unfortunate brothers ;
>   As a laundress tans her own face in the ray
>   To cleanse the garments of others."

It suggested a somewhat similar verse to my
own mind. Why should not our washerwoman's
work have its touch of poetry also? —

> This thought flashed by like a ray of light
>   That brightened my homely labor : —
> The water is making my own hands white
>   While I wash the robes of my neighbor.

And how delighted we were with Mrs. Kirk-
land's " A New Home: Who 'll Follow? " the
first real Western book I ever read. Its genuine
pioneer-flavor was delicious. And, moreover, it
was a prophecy to Sarah, Emilie, and myself, who
were one day thankful enough to find an " Aunty
Parshall's dish-kettle " in a cabin on an Illinois
prairie.

So the pleasantly occupied years slipped on,
I still nursing my purpose of a more systematic
course of study, though I saw no near possibility
of its fulfillment. It came in an unexpected way,
as almost everything worth having does come. I
could never have dreamed that I was going to
meet my opportunity nearly or quite a thousand
miles away, on the banks of the Mississippi. And

yet, with that strange, delightful consciousness of growth into a comprehension of one's self and of one's life that most young persons must occasionally have experienced, I often vaguely felt new heavens opening for my half-fledged wings to try themselves in. Things about me were good and enjoyable, but I could not quite rest in them; there was more for me to be, to know, and to do. I felt almost surer of the future than of the present.

If the dream of the millennium which brightened the somewhat sombre close of the first ten years of my life had faded a little, out of the very roughnesses of the intervening road light had been kindled which made the end of the second ten years glow with enthusiastic hope. I had early been saved from a great mistake; for it is the greatest of mistakes to begin life with the expectation that it is going to be easy, or with the wish to have it so. What a world it would be, if there were no hills to climb! Our powers were given us that we might conquer obstacles, and clear obstructions from the overgrown human path, and grow strong by striving, led onward always by an Invisible Guide.

Life to me, as I looked forward, was a bright blank of mystery, like the broad Western tracts of our continent, which in the atlases of those days bore the title of "Unexplored Regions." It was to be penetrated, struggled through; and its diffi-

culties were not greatly dreaded, for I had not
lost

> " The dream of Doing, —
> The first bound in the pursuing."

I knew that there was no joy like the joy of
pressing forward.

XII.

THE years between 1835 and 1845, which nearly cover the time I lived at Lowell, seem to me, as I look back at them, singularly interesting years. People were guessing and experimenting and wondering and prophesying about a great many things, — about almost everything. We were only beginning to get accustomed to steamboats and railroads. To travel by either was scarcely less an adventure to us younger ones than going up in a balloon.

Phrenology was much talked about; and numerous "professors" of it came around lecturing, and examining heads, and making charts of cranial "bumps." This was profitable business to them for a while, as almost everybody who invested in a "character" received a good one; while many very commonplace people were flattered into the belief that they were geniuses, or might be if they chose.

Mesmerism followed close upon phrenology; and this too had its lecturers, who entertained the stronger portion of their audiences by showing them how easily the weaker ones could be brought under an uncanny influence.

The most widespread delusion of the time was Millerism. A great many persons — and yet not so many that I knew even one of them — believed that the end of the world was coming in the year 1842; though the date was postponed from year to year, as the prophesy failed of fulfillment. The idea in itself was almost too serious to be jested about; and yet its advocates made it so literal a matter that it did look very ridiculous to unbelievers.

An irreverent little workmate of mine in the spinning-room made a string of jingling couplets about it, like this : —

> "Oh dear! oh dear! what shall we do
> In eighteen hundred and forty-two ?

> "Oh dear! oh dear! where shall we be
> In eighteen hundred and forty-three ?

> "Oh dear! oh dear! we shall be no more
> In eighteen hundred and forty-four.

> "Oh dear! oh dear! we sha' n't be alive
> In eighteen hundred and forty-five."

I thought it audacious in her, since surely she and all of us were aware that the world would come to an end some time, in some way, for every one of us. I said to myself that I could not have "made up" those rhymes. Nevertheless we all laughed at them together.

A comet appeared at about the time of the Miller excitement, and also a very unusual illumination of sky and earth by the Aurora Borealis. This latter occurred in midwinter. The whole heavens were of a deep rose-color — almost crimson — reddest at the zenith, and paling as it radiated towards the horizon. The snow was fresh on the ground, and that, too, was of a brilliant red. Cold as it was, windows were thrown up all around us for people to look out at the wonderful sight. I was gazing with the rest, and listening to exclamations of wonder from surrounding unseen beholders, when somebody shouted from far down the opposite block of buildings, with startling effect, —

> " You can't stand the fire
> In that great day ! "

It was the refrain of a Millerite hymn. The Millerites believed that these signs in the sky were omens of the approaching catastrophe. And it was said that some of them did go so far as to put on white "ascension robes," and assemble somewhere, to wait for the expected hour.

When daguerreotypes were first made, when we heard that the sun was going to take everybody's portrait, it seemed almost too great a marvel to be believed. While it was yet only a rumor that such a thing had been done, somewhere across the sea, I saw some verses about it which impressed me much, but which I only partly remember. These were the opening lines : —

> " Oh, what if thus our evil deeds
> Are mirrored on the sky,
> And every line of our wild lives
> Daguerreotyped on high ! "

My sister and I considered it quite an event when we went to have our daguerreotypes taken, just before we started for the West. The photograph was still an undeveloped mystery.

Things that looked miraculous then are commonplace now. It almost seems as if the children of to-day could not have so good a time as we did, science has left them so little to wonder about. Our attitude — the attitude of the time — was that of children climbing their dooryard fence, to watch an approaching show, and to conjecture what more remarkable spectacle could be following behind. New England had kept to the quiet old-fashioned ways of living for the first fifty years of the Republic. Now all was expectancy. Changes were coming. Things were going to happen, nobody could guess what.

Things have happened, and changes have come. The New England that has grown up with the last fifty years is not at all the New England that our fathers knew. We speak of having been reared under Puritanic influences, but the traditionary sternness of these was much modified, even in the childhood of the generation to which I belong. We did not recognize the grim features of the Puritan, as we used sometimes to read about him, in our parents or relatives. And yet we were children of the Puritans.

Everything that was new or strange came to us at Lowell. And most of the remarkable people of the day came also. How strange it was to see Mar Yohanan, a Nestorian bishop, walking through the factory yard in his Oriental robes with more than a child's wonder on his face at the stir and rush of everything! He came from Boston by railroad, and was present at a wedding at the clergyman's house where he visited. The rapidity of the simple Congregational service astonished him.

"What? marry on railroad, too?" he asked.

Dickens visited Lowell while I was there, and gave a good report of what he saw in his "American Notes." We did not leave our work even to gaze at distinguished strangers, so I missed seeing him. But a friend who did see him sketched his profile in pencil for me as he passed along the street. He was then best known as "Boz."

Many of the prominent men of the country were in the habit of giving Lyceum lectures, and the Lyceum lecture of that day was a means of education, conveying to the people the results of study and thought through the best minds. At Lowell it was more patronized by the mill-people than any mere entertainment. We had John

Quincy Adams, Edward Everett, John Pierpont, and Ralph Waldo Emerson among our lecturers, with numerous distinguished clergymen of the day. Daniel Webster was once in the city, trying a law case. Some of my girl friends went to the court-room and had a glimpse of his face, but I just missed seeing him.

Sometimes an Englishman, who was studying our national institutions, would call and have a friendly talk with us at our work. Sometimes it was a traveler from the South, who was interested in the same way. I remember one, an editor and author from Georgia, who visited our Improvement Circle, and who sent some of us "Offering" contributors copies of his books after he had returned home.

One of the pleasantest visitors that I recall was a young Quaker woman from Philadelphia, a school-teacher, who came to see for herself how the Lowell girls lived, of whom she had heard so much. A deep, quiet friendship grew up between us two. I wrote some verses for her when we parted, and she sent me one cordial, charmingly-written letter. In a few weeks I answered it; but the response was from another person, a near relative. She was dead. But she still remains a real person to me; I often recall her features and the tones of her voice. It was as if a beautiful spirit from an invisible world had slipped in among us, and quickly gone back again.

It was an event to me, and to my immediate friends among the mill-girls, when the poet Whittier came to Lowell to stay awhile. I had not supposed that it would be my good fortune to meet him; but one evening when we assembled at the "Improvement Circle," he was there. The "Offering" editor, Miss Harriet Farley, had lived in the same town with him, and they were old acquaintances.

It was a warm, summer evening. I recall the circumstance that a number of us wore white dresses; also that I shrank back into myself, and felt much abashed when some verses of mine were read by the editor, — with others so much better, however, that mine received little attention. I felt relieved; for I was not fond of having my productions spoken of, for good or ill. He commended quite highly a poem by another member of the Circle, on "Pentucket," the Indian name of his native place, Haverhill. My subject was "Sabbath Bells." As the Friends do not believe in "steeple-houses," I was at liberty to imagine that it was my theme, and not my verses, that failed to interest him.

Various other papers were read, — stories, sketches, etc., and after the reading there was a little conversation, when he came and spoke to me. I let the friend who had accompanied me do my part of the talking, for I was too much overawed by the presence of one whose poetry I had so long admired, to say a great deal. But from that evening we knew each other as friends; and, of course, the day has a white mark among the memories of my Lowell life.

Mr. Whittier's visit to Lowell had some political bearing upon the antislavery cause. It is strange now to think that a cause like that should not always have been our country's cause, — our country, — our own free nation! But antislavery sentiments were then regarded by many as traitorous heresies; and those who held them did not expect to win popularity. If the vote of the mill-girls had been taken, it would doubtless have been unanimous on the antislavery side. But those were also the days when a woman was not expected to give, or even to have, an opinion on subjects of public interest.

Occasionally a young girl was attracted to the Lowell mills through her own idealization of the life there, as it had been reported to her. Margaret Foley, who afterwards became distinguished as a sculptor, was one of these. She did not remain many months at her occupation, — which I think was weaving, — soon changing it for that of teaching and studying art. Those who came as she did were usually disappointed. Instead of an Arcadia, they found a place of matter-of-fact toil, filled with a company of industrious, wide-awake girls, who were faithfully improving their opportunities, while looking through them into avenues

toward profit and usefulness, more desirable yet.
It has always been the way of the steady-minded
New Englander to accept the present situation, —
but to accept it without boundaries, taking in also
the larger prospects — all the heavens above and
the earth beneath — towards which it opens.

The movement of New England girls toward
Lowell was only an impulse of a larger movement which about that time sent so many people
from the Eastern States into the West. The
needs of the West were constantly kept before us
in the churches. We were asked for contributions for Home Missions, which were willingly
given ; and some of us were appointed collectors
of funds for the education of indigent young men
to become Western Home Missionary preachers.
There was something almost pathetic in the read-
iness with which this was done by young girls
who were longing to fit themselves for teachers,
but had not the means. Many a girl at Lowell
was working to send her brother to college, who
had far more talent and character than he ; but
a man could preach, and it was not " orthodox "
to think that a woman could. And in her devotion to him, and her zeal for the spread of Christian truth, she was hardly conscious of her own
sacrifice. Yet our ministers appreciated the intelligence and piety of their feminine parishioners. An agent who came from the West for
school-teachers was told by our own pastor that

five hundred could easily be furnished from among Lowell mill-girls. Many did go, and they made another New England in some of our Western States.

The missionary spirit was strong among my companions. I never thought that I had the right qualifications for that work; but I had a desire to see the prairies and the great rivers of the West, and to get a taste of free, primitive life among pioneers.

Before the year 1845, several of my friends had emigrated as teachers or missionaries. One of the editors of the "Operatives' Magazine" had gone to Arkansas with a mill-girl who had worked beside her among the looms. They were at an Indian mission — to the Cherokees and Choctaws. I seemed to breathe the air of that far Southwest, in a spray of yellow jessamine which one of those friends sent me, pressed in a letter. People wrote very long letters then, in those days of twenty-five cent postage.

Rachel, at whose house our German class had been accustomed to meet, had also left her work, and had gone to western Virginia to take charge of a school. She wrote alluring letters to us about the scenery there; it was in the neighborhood of the Natural Bridge.

My friend Angeline, with whom I used to read "Paradise Lost," went to Ohio as a teacher, and returned the following year, — for a very brief visit, however, — and with a husband. Another acquaintance was in Wisconsin, teaching a pioneer school. Eliza, my intimate companion, was about to be married to a clergyman. She, too, eventually settled at the West.

The event which brought most change into my own life was the marriage of my sister Emilie. It involved the breaking up of our own little family, of which she had really been the " houseband," the return of my mother to my sisters at Beverly, and my going to board among strangers, as other girls did. I found excellent quarters and kind friends, but the home-life was ended.

My sister's husband was a grammar school master in the city, and their cottage, a mile or more out, among the open fields, was my frequent refuge from homesickness and the general clatter. Our partial separation showed me how much I had depended upon my sister. I had really let her do most of my thinking for me. Henceforth I was to trust to my own resources. I was no longer the " little sister " who could ask what to do, and do as she was told. It often brought me a feeling of dismay to find that I must make up my own mind about things small and great. And yet I was naturally self-reliant. I am not sure but self-reliance and dependence really belong together. They do seem to meet in the same character, like other extremes.

The health of Emilie's husband failing, after

a year or two, it was evident that he must change
his employment and his residence. He decided to
go with his brother to Illinois and settle upon a
prairie farm. Of course his wife and baby boy
must go too, and with the announcement of this
decision came an invitation to me to accompany
them. I had no difficulty as to my response. It
was just what I wanted to do. I was to teach a
district school; but what there was beyond that, I
could not guess. I liked to feel that it was all as
vague as the unexplored regions to which I was
going. My friend and room-mate Sarah, who
was preparing herself to be a teacher, was invited
to join us, and she was glad to do so. It was all
quickly settled, and early in the spring of 1846
we left New England.

When I came to a realization of what I was
leaving, when good-bys had to be said, I began
to feel very sorrowful, and to wish it was not to
be. I said positively that I should soon return,
but underneath my protestations I was afraid that
I might not. The West was very far off then, —
a full week's journey. It would be hard getting
back. Those I loved might die; I might die
myself. These thoughts passed through my mind,
though not through my lips. My eyes would
sometimes tell the story, however, and I fancy
that my tearful farewells must have seemed ridiculous to many of my friends, since my going was
of my own cheerful choice.

The last meeting of the Improvement Circle before I went away was a kind of surprise party to me. Several original poems were read, addressed to me personally. I am afraid that I received it all in a dumb, undemonstrative way, for I could not make it seem real that I was the person meant, or that I was going away at all. But I treasured those tributes of sympathy afterwards, under the strange, spacious skies where I sometimes felt so alone.

The editors of the "Offering" left with me a testimonial in money, accompanied by an acknowledgment of my contributions during several years; but I had never dreamed of pay, and did not know how to look upon it so. I took it gratefully, however, as a token of their appreciation, and twenty dollars was no small help toward my outfit. Friends brought me books and other keepsakes. Our minister gave me D'Aubigné's "History of the Reformation" as a parting gift. It was quite a circumstance to be "going out West."

The exhilaration of starting off on one's first long journey, young, ignorant, buoyant, expectant, is unlike anything else, unless it be youth itself, the real beginning of the real journey — life. Annoyances are overlooked. Everything seems romantic and dream-like.

We went by a southerly route, on account of starting so early in the season; there was snow on the ground the day we left. On the second day, after a moonlight night on Long Island Sound, we were floating down the Delaware, between shores misty-green with budding willows; then (most of us seasick, though I was not) we were tossed across Chesapeake Bay; then there was a railway ride to the Alleghanies, which gave us glimpses of the Potomac and the Blue Ridge, and of the lovely scenery around Harper's Ferry; then followed a stifling night on the mountains, when we were packed like sardines into a stage-coach, without a breath of air, and the passengers were cross because the baby cried, while I felt inwardly glad that one voice among us could give utterance to the general discomfort, my own part of which I could have borne if I could only have had an occasional peep out at the mountain-side. After that it was all river-voyaging, down the Monongahela into the Ohio, and up the Mississippi.

As I recall this part of it, I should say that it was the perfection of a Western journey to travel in early spring by an Ohio River steamboat, — such steamboats as they had forty years ago, comfortable, roomy, and well ordered. The company was social, as Western emigrants were wont to be when there were not so very many of them, and the shores of the river, then only thinly populated, were a constantly shifting panorama of wilderness beauty. I have never since seen a combination of spring colors so delicate as those shown by the uplifted forests of the Ohio, where the pure white of the dogwood and the peach-bloom tint of the red-bud (Judas tree) were contrasted with soft shades of green, almost endlessly various, on the unfolding leafage.

Contrasted with the Ohio, the Mississippi had nothing to show but breadth and muddiness. More than one of us glanced at its level shores, edged with a monotonous growth of cottonwood, and sent back a sigh towards the banks of the Merrimack. But we did not let each other know what the sigh was for, until long after. The breaking-up of our little company when the steamboat landed at Saint Louis was like the ending of a pleasant dream. We had to wake up to the fact that by striking due east thirty or forty miles across that monotonous greenness, we should reach our destination, and must accept whatever we should find there, with such grace as we could.

What we did find, and did not find, there is not room fully to relate here. Ours was at first the roughest kind of pioneering experience; such as persons brought up in our well-to-do New England could not be in the least prepared for, though they might imagine they were, as we did. We were dropped down finally upon a vast green expanse, extending hundreds of miles north and south through the State of Illinois, then known as Looking-Glass Prairie. The nearest cabin to

our own was about a mile away, and so small that
at that distance it looked like a shingle set up
endwise in the grass. Nothing else was in sight,
not even a tree, although we could see miles and
miles in every direction. There were only the
hollow blue heavens above us and the level green
prairie around us, — an immensity of intense
loneliness. We seldom saw a cloud in the sky,
and never a pebble beneath our feet. If we could
have picked up the commonest one, we should
have treasured it like a diamond. Nothing in
nature now seemed so beautiful to us as rocks.
We had never dreamed of a world without them;
it seemed like living on a floor without walls or
foundations.

After a while we became accustomed to the vast
sameness, and even liked it in a lukewarm way.
And there were times when it filled us with emo-
tions of grandeur. Boundlessness in itself is impressive; it makes us feel our littleness, and yet
releases us from that littleness.

The grass was always astir, blowing one way,
like the waves of the sea; for there was a steady,
almost an unvarying wind from the south. It
was like the sea, and yet even more wonderful,
for it was a sea of living and growing things.
The Spirit of God was moving upon the face of
the earth, and breathing everything into life. We
were but specks on the great landscape. But God
was above it all, penetrating it and us with his

infinite warmth. The distance from human beings made the Invisible One seem so near! Only
Nature and ourselves now, face to face with Him!

We could scarcely have found in all the world
a more complete contrast to the moving crowds
and the whir and dust of the City of Spindles,
than this unpeopled, silent prairie.

For myself, I know that I was sent in upon my
own thoughts deeper than I had ever been before.
I began to question things which I had never
before doubted. I must have reality. Nothing
but transparent truth would bear the test of this
great, solitary stillness. As the prairies lay open
to the sunshine, my heart seemed to lie bare beneath the piercing eye of the All-Seeing. I may
say with gratitude that only some superficial rubbish of acquired opinion was scorched away by
this searching light and heat. The faith of my
childhood, in its simplest elements, took firmer
root as it found broader room to grow in.

I had many peculiar experiences in my log-
cabin school-teaching, which was seldom more than
three months in one place. Only once I found
myself among New England people, and there I
remained a year or more, fairly reveling in a return to the familiar, thrifty ways that seem to
me to shape a more comfortable style of living
than any under the sun. " Vine Lodge " (so we
named the cottage for its embowering honey-
suckles), and its warm-hearted inmates, with my

little white schoolhouse under the oaks, make one of the brightest of my Western memories.

Only a mile or two away from this pretty retreat there was an edifice towards which I often looked with longing. It was a seminary for young women, probably at that time one of the best in the country, certainly second to none in the West. It had originated about a dozen years before, in a plan for Western collegiate education, organized by Yale College graduates. It was thought that women as well as men ought to share in the benefits of such a plan, and the result was Monticello Seminary. The good man whose wealth had made the institution a possibility lived in the neighborhood. Its trustees were of the best type of pioneer manhood, and its pupils came from all parts of the South and West.

Its Principal — I wonder now that I could have lived so near her for a year without becoming acquainted with her, — but her high local reputation as an intellectual woman inspired me with awe, and I was foolishly diffident. One day, however, upon the persuasion of my friends at Vine Lodge, who knew my wishes for a higher education, I went with them to call upon her. We talked about the matter which had been in my thoughts so long, and she gave me not only a cordial but an urgent invitation to come and enroll myself as a student. There were arrangements for those who could not incur the current expenses, to meet them by doing part of the domestic work, and of these I gladly availed myself. The stately limestone edifice, standing in the midst of an original growth of forest-trees, two or three miles from the Mississippi River, became my home — my student-home — for three years. The benefits of those three years I have been reaping ever since, I trust not altogether selfishly. It was always my desire and my ambition as a teacher, to help my pupils as my teachers had helped me.

The course of study at Monticello Seminary was the broadest, the most college-like, that I have ever known; and I have had experience since in several institutions of the kind. The study of mediæval and modern history, and of the history of modern philosophy, especially, opened new vistas to me. In these our Principal was also our teacher, and her method was to show us the tendencies of thought, to put our minds into the great current of human affairs, leaving us to collect details as we could, then or afterward. We came thus to feel that these were life-long studies, as indeed they are.

The course was somewhat elective, but her advice to me was, not to omit anything because I did not like it. I had a natural distaste for mathematics, and my recollections of my struggles with trigonometry and conic sections are not altogether those of a conquering heroine. But my teacher told me that my mind had need of just that exact sort of discipline, and I think she was right.

A habit of indiscriminate, unsystematized reading, such as I had fallen into, is entirely foreign to the scholarly habit of mind. Attention is the secret of real acquirement; but it was months before I could command my own attention, even when I was interested in the subject I was examining. It seemed as if all the pages of all the books I had ever read were turning themselves over between me and this one page that I wanted to understand. I found that mere reading does not by any means make a student.

It was more to me to come into communication with my wise teacher as a friend than even to receive the wisdom she had to impart. She was dignified and reticent, but beneath her reserve, as is often the case, was a sealed fountain of sympathy, which one who had the key could easily unlock. Thinking of her nobleness of character, her piety, her learning, her power, and her sweetness, it seems to me as if I had once had a Christian Zenobia or Hypatia for my teacher.

We speak with awed tenderness of our unseen guardian angels, but have we not all had our guiding angels, who came to us in visible form, and, recognized or unknown, kept beside us on our difficult path until they had done for us all that they could? It seems to me as if one had succeeded another by my side all through the years,

— always some one whose influence made my heart stronger and my way clearer; though sometimes it has been only a little child that came and laid its hand into my hand as if I were its guide, instead of its being mine.

My dear and honored Lady-Principal was surely one of my strong guiding angels, sent to meet me as I went to meet her upon my life-road, just at the point where I most needed her. For the one great thing she gave her pupils, — scope, — often quite left out of woman's education, — I especially thank her. The true education is to go on forever. But how can there be any hopeful going on without outlook? And having an infinite outlook, how can progress ever cease? It was worth while for me to go to those Western prairies, if only for the broader mental view that opened upon me in my pupilage there.

During my first year at the seminary I was appointed teacher of the Preparatory Department, — a separate school of thirty or forty girls, — with the opportunity to go on with my studies at the same time. It was a little hard, but I was very glad to do it, as I was unwilling to receive an education without rendering an equivalent, and I did not wish to incur a debt.

I believe that the postponement of these maturer studies to my early womanhood, after I had worked and taught, was a benefit to me. I had found out some of my special ignorances, what the things were which I most needed to know. I had learned that the book-knowledge I so much craved was not itself education, was not even culture, but only a help, an adjunct to both. As I studied more earnestly, I cared for fewer books, but those few made themselves indispensable. It still seems to me that in the Lowell mills, and in my log-cabin schoolhouse on the Western prairies, I received the best part of my early education.

The great advantage of a seminary course to me was that under my broad-minded Principal I learned what education really is: the penetrating deeper and rising higher into life, as well as making continually wider explorations; the rounding of the whole human being out of its nebulous elements into form, as planets and suns are rounded, until they give out safe and steady light. This makes the process an infinite one, not possible to be completed at any school.

Returning from the West immediately after my graduation, I was for ten years or so a teacher of young girls in seminaries much like my own Alma Mater. The best result to me of that experience has been the friendship of my pupils, — a happiness which must last as long as life itself.

A book must end somewhere, and the natural boundary of this narrative is drawn with my leaving New England for the West. I was to outline the story of my youth for the young, though I think many a one among them might tell a story far more interesting than mine. The most beautiful lives seldom find their way into print. Perhaps the most beautiful part of any life never does. I should like to flatter myself so.

I could not stay at the West. It was never really home to me there, and my sojourn of six or seven years on the prairies only deepened my love and longing for the dear old State of Massachusetts. I came back in the summer of 1852, and the unwritten remainder of my sketch is chiefly that of a teacher's and writer's experience ; regarding which latter I will add, for the gratification of those who have desired them, a few personal particulars.

While a student and teacher at the West I was still writing, and much that I wrote was published. A poem printed in "Sartain's Magazine," sent there at the suggestion of the editor of the "Lowell Offering," was the first for which I received remuneration — five dollars. Several poems written for the manuscript school journal at Monticello Seminary are in the "Household" collection of my verses, among them those entitled "Eureka," "Hand in Hand with Angels," and "Psyche at School." These, and various others written soon after, were printed in the "National Era," in return for which a copy of the paper was sent me. Nothing further was asked or expected.

The little song " Hannah Binding Shoes " —
written immediately after my return from the
West, — was a study from life — though not from
any one life — in my native town. It was brought
into notice in a peculiar way, — by my being ac-
cused of *stealing it*, by the editor of the magazine to which I had sent it with a request for the
usual remuneration, if accepted. Accidentally or
otherwise, this editor lost my note and signature,
and then denounced me by name in a newspaper
as a " literary thiefess ; " having printed the verses
with a *nom de plume* in his magazine without my
knowledge. It was awkward to have to come to
my own defense. But the curious incident gave
the song a wide circulation.

I did not attempt writing for money until it
became a necessity, when my health failed at
teaching, although I should long before then have
liked to spend my whole time with my pen, could
I have done so. But it was imperative that I
should have an assured income, however small ;
and every one who has tried it knows how uncer
tain a support one's pen is, unless it has become
very famous indeed. My life as a teacher, however, I regard as part of my best preparation for
whatever I have since written. I do not know
but I should recommend five or ten years of
teaching as the most profitable apprenticeship for
a young person who wished to become an author.
To be a good teacher implies self-discipline, and

a book written without something of that sort of personal preparation cannot be a very valuable one.

Success in writing may mean many different things. I do not know that I have ever reached it, except in the sense of liking better and better to write, and of finding expression easier. It is something to have won the privilege of going on. Sympathy and recognition are worth a great deal; the power to touch human beings inwardly and nobly is worth far more. The hope of attaining to such results, if only occasionally, must be a writer's best inspiration.

So far as successful publication goes, perhaps the first I considered so came when a poem of mine was accepted by the "Atlantic Monthly." Its title was "The Rose Enthroned," and as the poet Lowell was at that time editing the magazine I felt especially gratified. That and another poem, "The Loyal Woman's No," written early in the War of the Rebellion, were each attributed to a different person among our prominent poets, the "Atlantic" at that time not giving authors' signatures. Of course I knew the unlikeness; nevertheless, those who made the mistake paid me an unintentional compliment. Compliments, however, are very cheap, and by no means signify success. I have always regarded it as a better ambition to be a true woman than to become a successful writer. To be the second would never have seemed to me desirable, without also being the first.

In concluding, let me say to you, dear girls, for whom these pages have been written, that if I have learned anything by living, it is this, — that the meaning of life is education; not through book-knowledge alone, sometimes entirely without it. Education is growth, the development of our best possibilities from within outward; and it cannot be carried on as it should be except in a school, just such a school as we all find ourselves in — this world of human beings by whom we are surrounded. The beauty of belonging to this school is that we cannot learn anything in it by ourselves alone, but for and with our fellow-pupils, the wide earth over. We can never expect promotion here, except by taking our place among the lowest, and sharing their difficulties until they are removed, and we all become graduates together for a higher school.

Humility, Sympathy, Helpfulness, and Faith are the best teachers in this great university, and none of us are well educated who do not accept their training. The real satisfaction of living is, and must forever be, the education of all for each, and of each for all. So let us all try together to be good and faithful women, and not care too much for what the world may think of us or of our abilities !

My little story is not a remarkable one, for I

have never attempted remarkable things. In the words of one of our honored elder writers, given in reply to a youthful aspirant who had asked for some points of her "literary career," — "I never had a career."